CAMBRIDGE
Primary Computing

Learner's Book 3

Jon Chippindall,
Ben Davies & Isabella Lieghio

CAMBRIDGE
UNIVERSITY PRESS

Shaftesbury Road, Cambridge CB2 8EA, United Kingdom

One Liberty Plaza, 20th Floor, New York, NY 10006, USA

477 Williamstown Road, Port Melbourne, VIC 3207, Australia

314–321, 3rd Floor, Plot 3, Splendor Forum, Jasola District Centre, New Delhi – 110025, India

103 Penang Road, #05–06/07, Visioncrest Commercial, Singapore 238467

Cambridge University Press is part of the University of Cambridge.

It furthers the University's mission by disseminating knowledge in the pursuit of education, learning and research at the highest international levels of excellence.

www.cambridge.org
Information on this title: www.cambridge.org/9781009309226

© Cambridge University Press & Assessment 2024

This publication is in copyright. Subject to statutory exception and to the provisions of relevant collective licensing agreements, no reproduction of any part may take place without the written permission of Cambridge University Press.

20 19 18 17 16 15 14 13 12 11 10 9 8 7

Printed in Malaysia by Vivar Printing

A catalogue record for this publication is available from the British Library

ISBN 978-1-009-30922-6 Paperback with Digital Access (1 Year)
ISBN 978-1-009-32045-0 Digital Coursebook (1 Year)
ISBN 978-1-009-32046-7 eBook

Additional resources for this publication at www.cambridge.org/go

Cambridge University Press has no responsibility for the persistence or accuracy of URLs for external or third-party internet websites referred to in this publication, and does not guarantee that any content on such websites is, or will remain, accurate or appropriate. Information regarding prices, travel timetables, and other factual information given in this work is correct at the time of first printing but Cambridge University Press does not guarantee the accuracy of such information thereafter.

....

NOTICE TO TEACHERS IN THE UK
It is illegal to reproduce any part of this work in material form (including photocopying and electronic storage) except under the following circumstances:
(i) where you are abiding by a licence granted to your school or institution by the Copyright Licensing Agency;
(ii) where no such licence exists, or where you wish to exceed the terms of a licence, and you have gained the written permission of Cambridge University Press;
(iii) where you are allowed to reproduce without permission under the provisions of Chapter 3 of the Copyright, Designs and Patents Act 1988, which covers, for example, the reproduction of short passages within certain types of educational anthology and reproduction for the purposes of setting examination questions.

....

Endorsement statement

Endorsement indicates that a resource has passed Cambridge International's rigorous quality-assurance process and is suitable to support the delivery of a Cambridge International curriculum framework. However, endorsed resources are not the only suitable materials available to support teaching and learning, and are not essential to be used to achieve the qualification. Resource lists found on the Cambridge International website will include this resource and other endorsed resources.

Any example answers to questions taken from past question papers, practice questions, accompanying marks and mark schemes included in this resource have been written by the authors and are for guidance only. They do not replicate examination papers. In examinations the way marks are awarded may be different. Any references to assessment and/or assessment preparation are the publisher's interpretation of the curriculum framework requirements. Examiners will not use endorsed resources as a source of material for any assessment set by Cambridge International.

While the publishers have made every attempt to ensure that advice on the qualification and its assessment is accurate, the official curriculum framework, specimen assessment materials and any associated assessment guidance materials produced by the awarding body are the only authoritative source of information and should always be referred to for definitive guidance. Cambridge International recommends that teachers consider using a range of teaching and learning resources based on their own professional judgement of their students' needs.

Cambridge International has not paid for the production of this resource, nor does Cambridge International receive any royalties from its sale. For more information about the endorsement process, please visit www.cambridgeinternational.org/endorsed-resources

Cambridge International copyright material in this publication is reproduced under licence and remains the intellectual property of Cambridge Assessment International Education.

Third party websites and resources referred to in this publication have not been endorsed by Cambridge Assessment International Education.

Introduction

Welcome to Stage 3 of Cambridge Primary Computing!

Technology is a big part of how we live our lives today.

This book will help you to find out more about the technology we see and use all around us.

There are lots of fun and interesting activities in this book to get you thinking about how technology works.

You will find out:

- why making mistakes helps us become better programmers
- how putting data into a spreadsheet can help to keep it organised
- what the World Wide Web is
- how robots can help us to complete tasks
- which everyday devices can be connected to the internet.

You will write messages using secret codes, learn how to program a tiny computer called a BBC micro:bit, and design your own bedroom of the future.

Doing the activities with a partner and talking about what you find out will help you to learn even more about computing.

We hope that you enjoy discovering all about technology around us!

Jon Chippindall, Ben Davies and Isabella Lieghio

Contents

How to use this book — 6

1 Computational thinking and programming
1.1 Everyday algorithms — 9
1.2 Inputs and outputs — 34
1.3 Introducing Scratch — 46
1.4 Moving and changing sprites — 65
1.5 Clear and concise programs — 76
1.6 Introducing the micro:bit — 85

2 Managing data
2.1 How data can help us — 105
2.2 Super spreadsheets — 117

3 Networks and digital communication
3.1 Networks everywhere! — 142
3.2 Secret ciphers — 157

4 Computer systems
4.1 Hardware and software working together — 171
4.2 The role of robots — 182
4.3 Inputs and outputs around us — 195

Glossary — 210
Acknowledgements — 218

> Note for teachers: Throughout the resource there is a symbol to indicate where additional digital only content is provided. This content can be accessed through the Digital Learner's Book on Cambridge GO. It can be launched either from the Media tab or directly from the page. The symbol that denotes additional digital content is: 🗗.
> The source files can also be downloaded from the Source files tab on Cambridge GO. In addition, this tab contains a teacher guidance document which supports the delivery of digital activities and programming tasks in this Learner's Book.

How to use this book

How to use this book

In this book you will find lots of different features to help your learning.

What you will learn in the topic. ⟶

> **We are going to:**
> - learn how inputs (information or data) can be used to start algorithms
> - find inputs in algorithms

Important words to learn. ⟶

> algorithms   inputs
> data   outputs

A reminder about what you already know and an activity to start you off. ⟶

> **Getting started**
> **What do you already know?**
> - You can follow algorithms to help you do everyday tasks.
> - Finding and fixing mistakes in algorithms is called debugging.
> - Input means to send something into a digital device.

Fun activities about computing. Sometimes, you will use a computer. ⟶

> **Activity 4**
> **Spell it out**
> You will need:
> a pencil and paper or a whiteboard pen and mini whiteboard, source file **1.1_spell_it_out**
>
> Zara is playing a game.
> She has to make words from the letters in a grid.
>
> | m | | e | p |
> |---|---|---|---|
> | Start | | r | s |

Some activities do not need a computer. These are called unplugged activities. They help you to understand important ideas about computing. ⟶

> **Unplugged activity 1**
> **Following theme park algorithms**
> You will need:
> a pencil and paper or a whiteboard pen and mini whiteboard
>
> Sofia wants to visit a theme park.
> She decides to plan the trip.
> First, Sofia looks at a map of the theme park.

Sometimes, you will see this question. It will help you to think about your work. ⟶

> **How am I doing?**
> If you can explain how you thought logically about the most sensible way to give these instructions, draw a star in your book.
> If you found it difficult to think about a sensible order for these instructions, find someone who has drawn a star in their book.
> Ask: how did you decide which instruction to put first?

How to use this book

Tasks to help you to practise what you have learnt.

Programming tasks are in Unit 1.

> **Programming task 2**
> **Adding 'wait' commands**
> You will need:
> a desktop computer, laptop or tablet with access to Scratch, source file **1.5_wait_commands**
>
> Open Scratch and open the file your teacher gives you.
> Look at the program. How many costumes are used?
> **Step 1:** Run the program by clicking on the green flag above the stage area.
> How many different costumes did you see?

Practical tasks are in Unit 2.

> **Practical task 1**
> **Entering Sofia's data into a spreadsheet**
> You will need:
> a desktop computer, laptop or tablet, a spreadsheet program (for example, Microsoft Excel), source file **2.1_hobbies**
>
> Open the file your teacher gives you.
> It has the table headings that Sofia has already entered.
> Enter the different hobbies and the number of children choosing each hobby as their favourite.

Look out for this icon. You are going to do an activity at the computer using a source file or website link. This content can be found in the Digital Learner's Book on Cambridge GO. Your teacher will help you to get started.

Questions that help you to check that you understand the topic. Are you ready to move on?

> **Questions**
> 1 Which command blocks has Arun combined?
> 2 Which instruction has Arun used instead?
> 3 Will the sprite still move the same number of steps?

Things to remember when you are using a computer.

> **Stay safe!**
> The data Marcus has collected is personal data.
> Marcus should keep this data safe and not share it with anyone.
> When you are online, always ask an adult before sharing personal data.

Interesting facts connected to the topic.

> **Did you know?**
> Computer systems can automatically open and close windows depending on the temperature.
> The windows in this greenhouse open when it is too hot inside.

How to use this book

Questions to help you think about how you learn.

> You have used algorithms that use words and algorithms that use pictures.
> Which do you find more useful?
> Why do you find this type of algorithm more useful?

What you have learnt in the topic.

Look what I can do!
- ☐ I know that inputs can be used to start algorithms.
- ☐ I can find the inputs in algorithms.
- ☐ I understand what the output of an algorithm is.
- ☐ I can write algorithms that use inputs to create outputs.

At the end of each unit, there is a project for you to carry out, using what you have learnt. You might make something or solve a problem.

Project

Showing feelings on the micro:bit

You will need:
a desktop computer or laptop, a micro:bit, a micro USB B cable and access to the MakeCode website; or a tablet, a micro:bit, a battery pack and access to the MakeCode app, printout of source file **1.13_microbit_grid**, colouring pen or pencil, a pencil and paper or a whiteboard pen and mini whiteboard

Have you ever been in a lesson where you did not understand something?

Have you felt worried about telling your teacher that you did not understand in front of your classmates?

If the answer is yes, do not worry. Lots of children feel the same way.

However, it is really useful for your teacher to know how confident you feel with the learning

Questions that cover what you have learnt in the unit. If you can answer these, you are ready to move on to the next unit.

Check your progress

1. Which **two** of these problems could be solved by collecting data?
   - A choosing which biscuits to buy for a party
   - B creating a cake for a party
   - C deciding which games to play at a party
2. What data would you collect to help solve the problems you chose in question 1?
3. Write the name of each coloured cell in this spreadsheet.

1 > Computational thinking and programming

> ## 1.1 Everyday algorithms

We are going to:

- follow and use simple algorithms
- make changes to algorithms
- find and fix mistakes in algorithms
- understand what logical thinking is and how it can help us to write algorithms
- predict the outcome of an algorithm that has been changed
- learn why it is helpful to split tasks (jobs) into smaller parts
- identify repeated steps in tasks
- understand the importance of algorithms being clear and concise.

algorithm
concise
debug
editing
logical thinking
precise
predictions
repeat
tasks

1   Computational thinking and programming

Getting started

What do you already know?

- An algorithm is a set of instructions in a sequence.
- Algorithms can help you to make something, do something or get somewhere.
- Finding and fixing errors in algorithms is called debugging.

Now try this!

Look at these shapes. They make a pattern, which means that they repeat in a certain way.

Arun has started writing an algorithm so that someone else can draw the same pattern.

Can you complete the algorithm?

Look carefully at what shapes to draw.

1 Draw a red triangle.
2 Draw a blue triangle to the right.
3 Draw a red square to the right.
4 Draw a blue square to the right.
5 Draw a red circle to the right.

1.1 Everyday algorithms

Using algorithms

There are lots of different types of **algorithms**.

An algorithm is a set of instructions.

Algorithms can help you to make something, like following a recipe.

Algorithms can help you to do something, like connecting a piece of hardware to your computer.

Algorithms can help you to get somewhere, like following directions to the library.

Algorithms should be easy to follow. If algorithms are confusing, people will not be able to use them.

You have used algorithms written with symbols, like arrows.

You have also used algorithms written with words.

Unplugged activity 1

Following theme park algorithms

> You will need:
> a pencil and paper or a whiteboard pen and mini whiteboard

Sofia wants to visit a theme park.

She decides to plan the trip.

First, Sofia looks at a map of the theme park.

11

1 Computational thinking and programming

Continued

The map shows her where the rides and other places can be found.

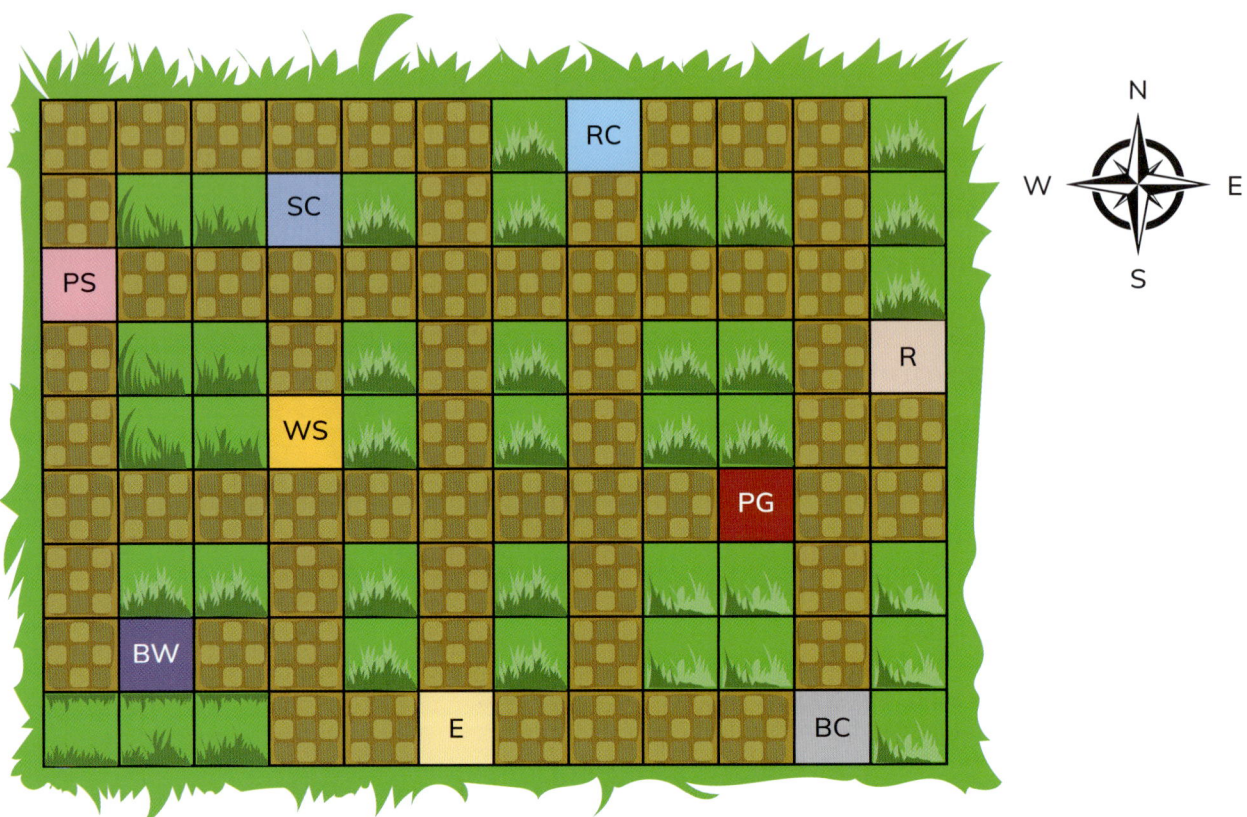

PS = Pirate ship    RC = Rollercoaster

BW = Big wheel    PG = Playground

SC = Spinning cups    BC = Bumper cars

WS = Water slide    R = Restaurant

E = Entrance

Continued

> The map has a compass. I will use this to help me get around the park. The four main points on a compass are: north (N), south (S), east (E) and west (W).

Sofia decides to write some algorithms.

These give directions for how to get from one part of the theme park to another part.

Sofia's algorithms use compass directions. 'Face east' means to point in the same direction as the 'E' on the compass.

The algorithm below gives Sofia directions to get from the entrance to her first two places.

Follow Sofia's algorithm.

Sofia's first algorithm

1. Face east.
2. Go forward 5 squares.
3. Face north.
4. Go forward 3 squares.
5. Face west.
6. Go forward 1 square.

1 Computational thinking and programming

Continued

1 Which place did Sofia visit first?

2 Which place did Sofia visit next?

3 Below are three more of Sofia's algorithms.

They give directions to get from the pirate ship to another place.

Match each algorithm to the place it gives directions to.

A the restaurant

B the playground

C the bumper cars

Algorithm 1	Algorithm 2	Algorithm 3
1 Face east.	1 Face east.	1 Face south.
2 Go forward 3 squares.	2 Go forward 10 squares.	2 Go forward 3 squares.
3 Face south.	3 Face south.	3 Face east.
4 Go forward 6 squares.	4 Go forward 1 square.	4 Go forward 9 squares.
5 Face east.	5 Face east.	
6 Go forward 7 squares.	6 Go forward 1 square.	

1.1 Everyday algorithms

Editing algorithms

Sometimes, if an algorithm isn't working correctly, you may need to change it.

Another word for this is **editing**.

You might not need to edit the whole algorithm.

You can split the algorithm into parts and only edit the parts that are wrong, or the parts that you want to change.

Unplugged activity 2

Editing theme park algorithms

> You will need:
> a pencil and paper or a whiteboard pen and mini whiteboard

Sofia has just been on the water slide.

Next, she wants to go on the rollercoaster.

However, Sofia's algorithm got wet and she cannot read some of the instructions.

15

1 Computational thinking and programming

Continued

Sofia has tried to remember what her algorithm said.

She has written it out again. But she has made a mistake.

1   Use the map to work out Sofia's mistake.

Remember, she is starting from the water slide and she wants to get to the rollercoaster.

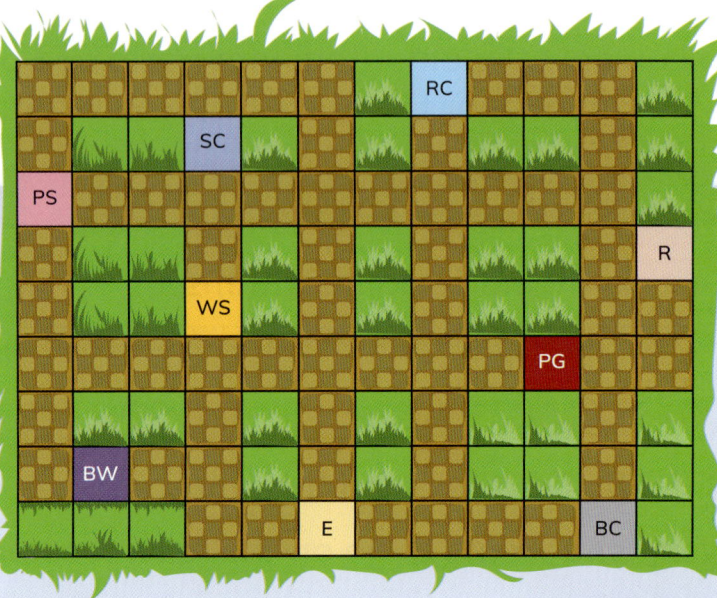

1   Face north.
2   Go forward 2 squares.
3   Face west.
4   Go forward 4 squares.
5   Face north.
6   Go forward 2 squares.

Marcus is also planning to visit the theme park.

He starts with Sofia's first algorithm, which starts at the entrance.

However, Marcus wants to make some changes because he wants to go to different places.

Marcus still wants to go from the entrance to the bumper cars, but he wants to finish at the restaurant.

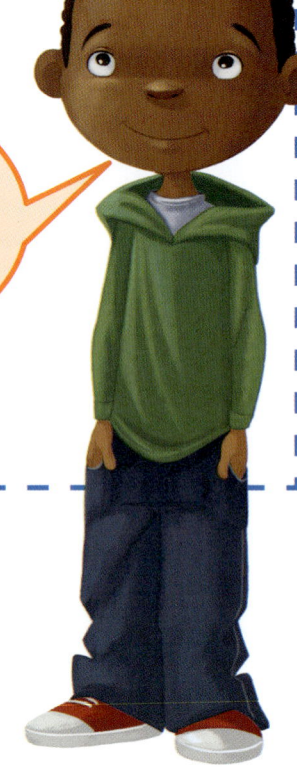

I keep the instructions that I need and change the instructions I do not need.

1.1 Everyday algorithms

Continued

2 Copy out Sofia's algorithm.

Change the part you need to.

It must give directions from the entrance to the bumper cars, and then to the restaurant.

> 1 Face east.
> 2 Go forward 5 squares.
> 3 Face north.
> 4 Go forward 3 squares.
> 5 Face west.
> 6 Go forward 1 square.

How am I doing?

How did you decide which instructions to keep?

How did you decide which instructions to add?

Discuss your answers with a partner.
Did you do things the same way?

1 Computational thinking and programming

Logical thinking

When you use information to make decisions, you are using **logical thinking**.

Logical thinking is when you think of sensible ideas to help solve a problem.

Zara and Marcus are going to spend the whole day in the park.

They explain what they have packed for their trip.

Marcus has thought about what the weather is going to be like in the afternoon, not just the morning.

He used this information to decide he should take a coat.

Marcus has used logical thinking.

> It is sunny this morning so I am packing a sun hat.

> I am packing a sun hat and a coat because I have checked the weather forecast and it will rain this afternoon.

18

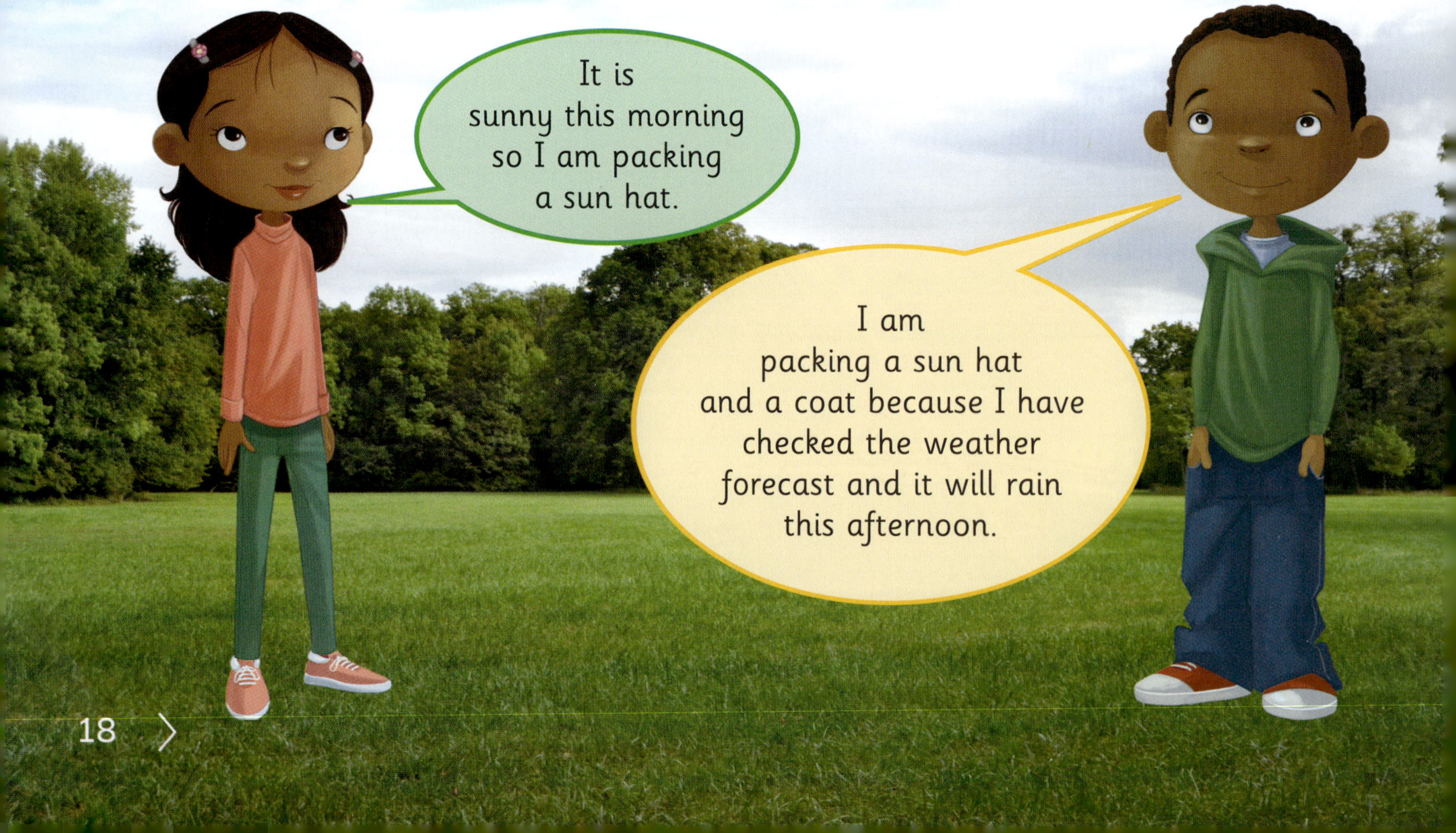

1.1 Everyday algorithms

You can use logical thinking when you write algorithms.

Think about all the steps someone will need to follow.

It also helps to think about the order that the steps should be in.

For example, if you want to write a recipe for baking a cake, you need to think about:

- what ingredients to use
- what equipment to use
- what temperature the oven needs to be
- what instructions need to be followed
- what order the instructions are given in.

Logical thinking will help you write algorithms that are **precise** (clear and correct) and easy to follow.

When logical thinking is not used, people might not put the steps in the most sensible order.

When instructions are not in the most sensible order, it can take longer to complete the algorithm.

Arun has had to stop baking because he does not have any eggs.

He should have checked he had all the ingredients first.

The steps were not in the most sensible order.

1 Computational thinking and programming

Unplugged activity 3

Dirty dishes

> You will need:
> a pencil and paper or a whiteboard pen and mini whiteboard

Zara wants to write an algorithm to help someone do the washing up.

The steps that need to be followed are shown below.

We will look at how to split an algorithm into smaller steps later.

This time, Zara has done it for you. However, the steps are not in the correct order.

Work with a partner. Use logical thinking.

Write the instructions in the correct order.

- Dry the plate with a tea towel.
- Fill the sink with water and washing-up liquid.
- Put the dry plate away.
- Put any food in the bin.
- Get a dirty plate.
- Put the plate in the water and clean it.

1.1 Everyday algorithms

> **Continued**
>
> **How am I doing?**
>
> If you can explain how you thought logically about the most sensible way to give these instructions, draw a star in your book.
>
> If you found it difficult to think about a sensible order for these instructions, find someone who has drawn a star in their book.
>
> Ask: how did you decide which instruction to put first?

Making predictions

When people make **predictions**, they use what they already know to suggest what might happen.

You might have made predictions about some of the following:

- what might happen next in a story
- the result of a science experiment
- who will win a sports competition.

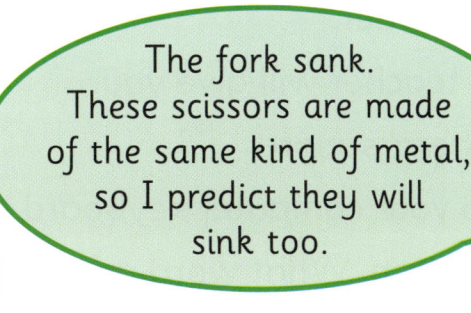

The fork sank. These scissors are made of the same kind of metal, so I predict they will sink too.

When you make predictions, you are using logical thinking.

1   Computational thinking and programming

This is because you are using what you have already learnt to make sensible decisions about what might happen.

You can use predictions when you have an algorithm to follow.

People often read through the algorithm first to help them understand what they need to do.

They also predict what will happen when they follow the algorithm.

Activity 4

Spell it out

> You will need:
> a pencil and paper or a whiteboard pen and mini whiteboard, source file **1.1_spell_it_out**

Zara is playing a game.

She has to make words from the letters in a grid.

Each time she starts on the green square and writes an algorithm to collect the letters in order.

Open the file your teacher will give you.

Click in the 'Start here' square.

	m		e	p
Start here		r		s
	t		g	
		a		c

Use the arrows on your computer keyboard to move around the grid.

Follow Zara's algorithm. What word does she spell?

 Collect letter.

⬅ ⬅ Collect letter.

⬆ ⬅ Collect letter.

Zara wants to make a new word.

1.1 Everyday algorithms

Continued

She does not write a new algorithm.

Zara makes changes to her first algorithm.

➡➡➡➡ ⬇⬇ Collect letter.

⬅⬅ Collect letter.

⬆ ⬆ Collect letter.

➡➡ Collect letter.

Explaining why you made your predictions shows you have used logical thinking and used what you already know.

Look at the changes that Zara has made to her algorithm.

She has crossed out some arrows and added new arrows to show the changes she has made.

Step 1: Make the following predictions.

a How many letters will the word have?

b How many of these letters will be the same as the first word?

c How many letters will be different from the first word?

Share your predictions with a partner.

If you and your partner made different predictions, explain your reasons for making that prediction.

Now check your predictions. Use the grid in the source file to find out the new word that Zara has made.

Step 2: Copy Zara's original algorithm. Then edit it to make each of the following words:

a cap
b care
c cage.

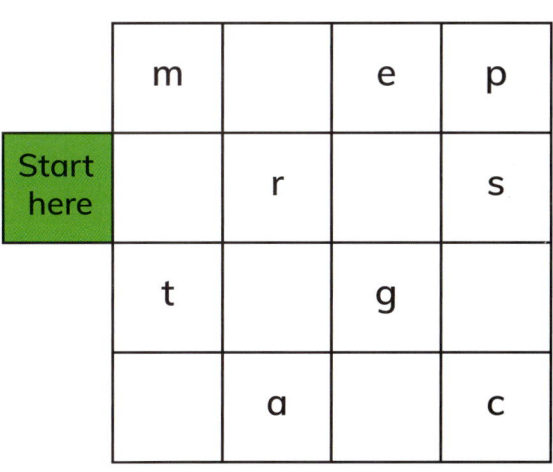

1 Computational thinking and programming

Splitting algorithms into smaller steps

When people have complex **tasks** (jobs) to complete, they often split the task into smaller steps.

This makes it easier to complete the task.

Organising a school play is a complex task.

It can be split into smaller steps such as:

- writing the script
- thinking up some songs
- making the costumes
- practising the play
- telling parents about the play.

Different people can do different parts of the task. This means someone only needs to understand their part of the task.

It is useful if there is a problem. If you find a problem when you are making the costumes, only that step needs to be corrected.

If the steps are in the right order, it makes the task easier to follow.

Let's look at some reasons why it is useful to split a task into smaller steps.

When you write algorithms, you can also split them into smaller steps. Then you can write an algorithm for each smaller step.

Question

1   An algorithm to help someone tidy their bedroom could be split into these smaller steps:

    Step 1 Pick things up off the floor.

    Step 2 Put away clothes.

    Imagine you are writing an algorithm for each of these small steps. Match each instruction below with the small step that you think it belongs to. You should do this by writing the number of the step and then the letter of the instruction.

    A   Put rubbish in the bin.

    B   Put socks in the drawer.

Marcus's morning

A precise algorithm often has lots of different steps.

For example, an algorithm for getting ready for school could have a hundred different tasks.

This could become quite confusing!

Marcus has been rushing to get ready for school in the morning.

1 Computational thinking and programming

Marcus decides to write an algorithm to help him to be more organised.

He wants to split his 'getting ready' algorithm into smaller steps.

To do this, he writes down all the tasks he does when he is getting ready.

> **Marcus's 'Get ready' algorithm**
> - Get dressed
> - Eat breakfast
> - Brush my teeth
> - Wash my face
> - Pack my school bag
> - Travel to school

1.1 Everyday algorithms

Unplugged activity 5

Getting ready for school

> You will need:
> a pencil and paper or a whiteboard pen and mini whiteboard

Zara has helped Marcus by writing one of the smaller parts of his 'Get ready' algorithm.

She has written the algorithm for washing his face.

1. Get your face wash and a face cloth.
2. Put some warm water in the sink.
3. Rinse your face with the water.
4. Wet the face cloth and put the face wash on it.
5. Rub the face cloth across your face.
6. Rinse your face and the face cloth with the water.
7. Remove water from the sink.
8. Put the face cloth somewhere to dry.
9. Put the face wash away.

> Zara's algorithm is really useful because it tells me what I need, what to do and where things should go when I have finished.

1 Computational thinking and programming

> **Continued**
>
> Write an algorithm for the 'Eat breakfast' section of Marcus's 'Get ready' algorithm.
>
> Marcus likes to eat cereal and have a glass of orange juice.
>
> Remember to tell Marcus what he needs, what to do and where to put things when he has finished.

Editing a part of the algorithm

When algorithms are split into smaller parts, it makes it easier to edit them.

Marcus usually walks to school, but he is planning to ride his bike to school next week.

This means he needs to edit his 'Get ready' algorithm.

However, he only needs to edit the 'travel to school' part of his algorithm.

The 'travel to school' part of his 'Get ready' algorithm is shown below.

1. Put my coat on.
2. Pick up my rucksack.
3. Open the front door.
4. Walk through the open doorway.
5. Close the front door.
6. Walk to school.

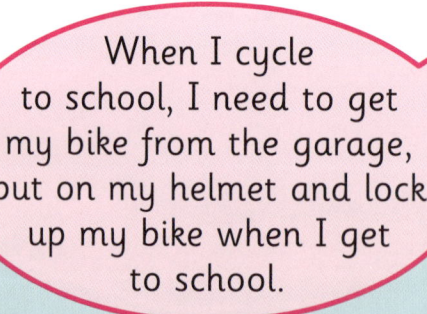

When I cycle to school, I need to get my bike from the garage, put on my helmet and lock up my bike when I get to school.

1.1 Everyday algorithms

Question

2 Edit the 'travel to school' part of Marcus's 'Get ready' algorithm so he can use it to ride his bike to school.

It would have been more difficult to edit the algorithm if it was not already split into smaller parts.

Did you know?

When you make a computer game, the task is split into smaller parts. These parts include:

- designing the characters and the setting
- creating the story for the game
- writing the computer program
- testing the program.

Unplugged activity 6

Present wrapping

You will need:
a pencil and paper or a whiteboard pen and mini whiteboard

Zara has written an algorithm to wrap presents.

She split the task into smaller parts and wrote an algorithm for each part.

As you read it, see if you can spot any problems or errors in Zara's algorithm.

29

1 Computational thinking and programming

Continued

Choosing the wrapping paper
1. Collect all the wrapping paper that you have.
2. Pick the wrapping paper that you think the person will like the most.
3. Put all the other wrapping paper away.

Preparing the wrapping paper
4. Unroll the wrapping paper you have chosen.
5. Get a piece of the paper that is big enough to cover the present.

Wrapping the present
6. Put the present in the middle of the wrapping paper.
7. Fold the sides up until they meet.

Adding decorations
8. Place a piece of ribbon around the wrapped present.
9. Stick a bow on the wrapping paper.

Zara's friends have tried to use this algorithm, but they have not been able to wrap a present. This is because the algorithm is not very precise.

Work with a partner and look at the problems each person faced.

1.1 Everyday algorithms

> **Continued**
>
> For each problem, decide which part of the algorithm you will need to **debug**.
>
> Debugging means finding and fixing errors.
>
>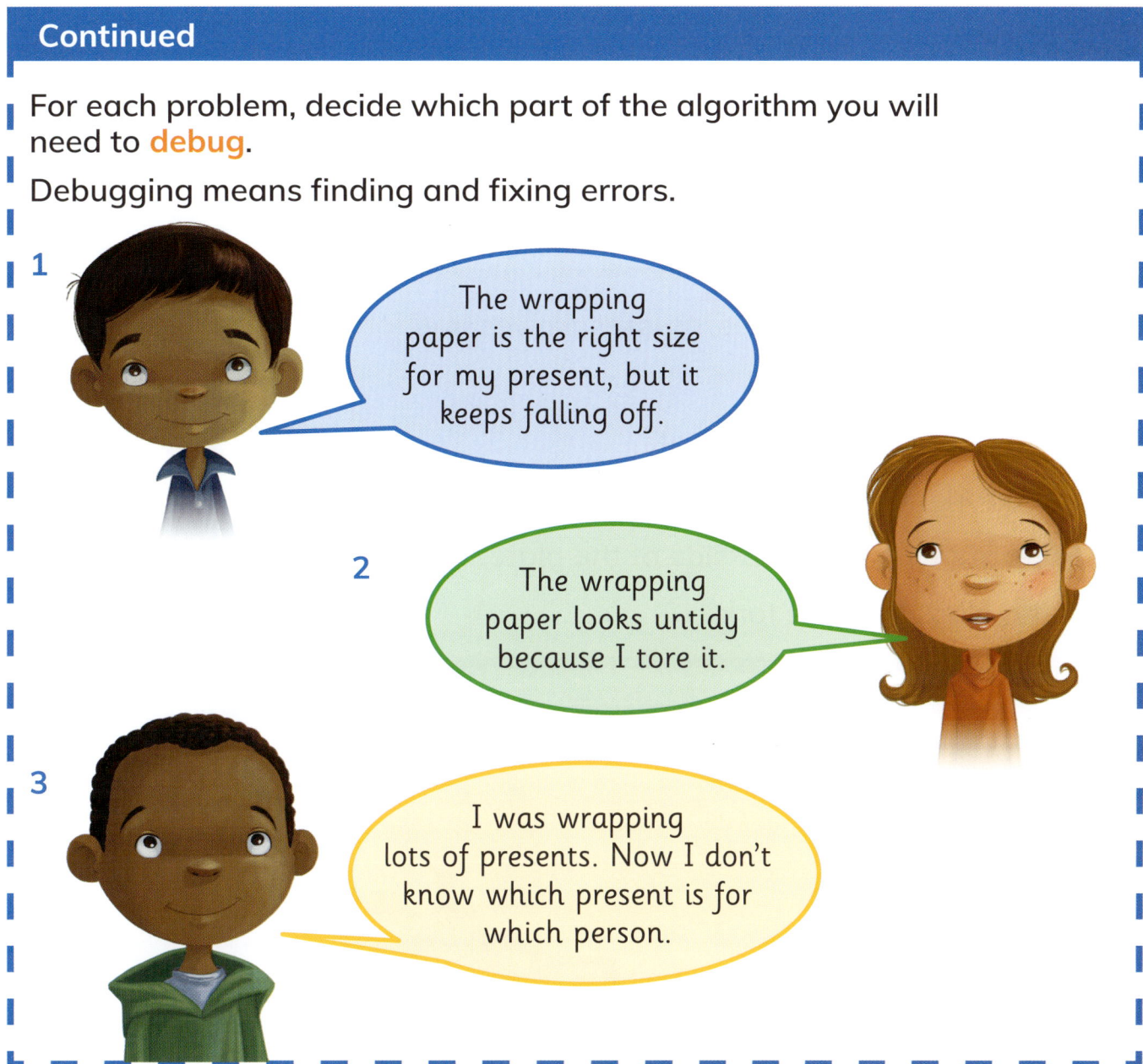
>
> 1. The wrapping paper is the right size for my present, but it keeps falling off.
>
> 2. The wrapping paper looks untidy because I tore it.
>
> 3. I was wrapping lots of presents. Now I don't know which present is for which person.

Concise algorithms

When you are planning to write algorithms, it is useful to think about any steps that you need to **repeat** (do again and again).

If you were following the algorithm for wrapping presents in the last activity and you were using the same wrapping paper, you could repeat steps 4–9 each time you wrapped a new present.

1 Computational thinking and programming

Question

3   Look at the steps below.

They are from an algorithm to help someone get ready for a meal.

Which steps need to be repeated?

1 Get out four mats, plates, glasses, knives and forks.
2 Put a mat on the table.
3 Put a plate on top of the mat.
4 Put a fork on one side of the plate.
5 Put a knife on the other side of the plate.
6 Put a glass near the fork.
7 Sit down.

Finding the steps that will be repeated in a task is useful because it allows you to write a more **concise** algorithm. Concise means not using extra words when you do not need them.

1.1 Everyday algorithms

Instead of writing the instructions out several times, you can tell the person to repeat the instructions.

This means you can have a more concise algorithm.

Remember, concise algorithms do not repeat words or instructions.

Look what I can do!

- ☐ I can follow and use simple algorithms.
- ☐ I can make changes to algorithms.
- ☐ I can find and fix mistakes in algorithms.
- ☐ I understand what logical thinking is and how it can help me to write algorithms.
- ☐ I can predict the output of an algorithm that has been changed.
- ☐ I can explain why splitting a task into smaller steps is helpful.
- ☐ I can identify repeated steps in tasks.
- ☐ I understand the importance of algorithms being clear and concise.

1 Computational thinking and programming

> 1.2 Inputs and outputs

We are going to:

- learn how inputs (information or data) can be used to start algorithms
- find inputs in algorithms
- understand what happens when an algorithm is followed (the output)
- write algorithms that use inputs to create outputs.

> algorithms inputs
> data outputs

Getting started

What do you already know?

- You can follow algorithms to help you do everyday tasks.
- Finding and fixing mistakes in algorithms is called debugging.
- Input means to send something into a digital device.
- Output is when a digital device sends out information.

1.2 Inputs and outputs

Continued

Now try this!

Arun and Sofia have each written an algorithm.

Both algorithms tell you how to draw a stick person.

Arun and Sofia have different ideas about what the stick person should look like.

Their algorithms are both correct, but their stick people will look different.

Arun's algorithm
1   Draw a circle for the head.
2   Draw a straight line for the body.
3   Draw two straight lines for the arms.
4   Draw two straight lines for the legs.

Sofia's algorithm
1   Use a red pencil to draw a circle for the head.
2   Use a blue pencil to draw a straight line for the body.
3   Use a green pencil to draw two straight lines for the arms.
4   Use an orange pencil to draw two straight lines for the legs.

Think about what will be drawn if you follow these two algorithms.
- What will be the same?
- What will be different?

Follow the algorithms to draw the stick people if it helps you.

35

1 Computational thinking and programming

Inputs in algorithms

We have already looked at input devices.

Remember, an input device sends an input to the computer.
An **input** is information.

Here are some input devices that can send information into a computer:

- a mouse
- a keyboard
- a tablet screen.

When we write algorithms, we do not use input devices to send an input.

The information is received by us.

When we receive that information, we know that we should follow the rest of the instructions in the algorithm.

When we are talking about algorithms, the input is the information that tells us to follow the instructions.

When we hear a school bell ring, it tells us to do something, such as go to lunch.

The school bell ringing is the input.

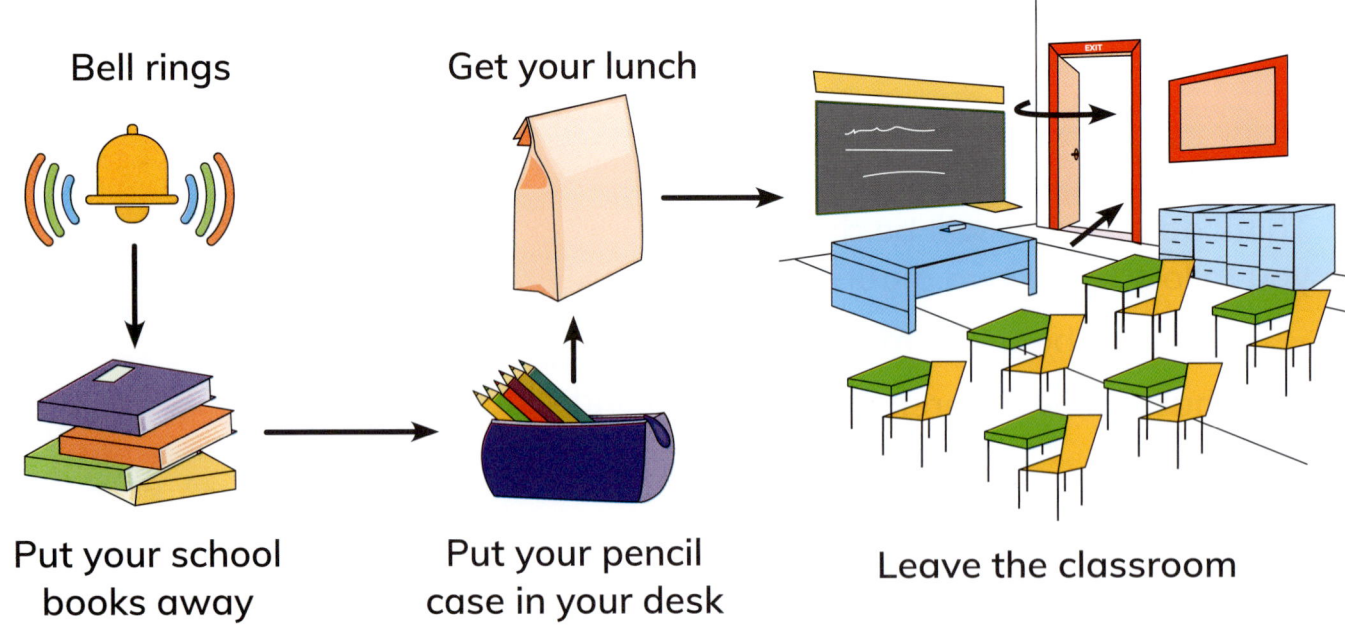

Bell rings → Put your school books away → Put your pencil case in your desk → Get your lunch → Leave the classroom

36

1.2 Inputs and outputs

Inputs in algorithms can be:

- something you hear (such as an alarm clock)
- something you see (such as a flag being waved)
- something you feel (such as your shoulder being tapped).

We are going to look at algorithms that use inputs to control when someone starts following the instructions.

Inputs in everyday algorithms

The algorithm below shows how to play a hiding game.

One algorithm is for the players who are hiding.

The other algorithm is for the person who is finding the others.

Algorithm for hiding
1. Start when you hear the finder start to count.
2. Find a hiding place.
3. Hide there.

Algorithm for finding
1. Start when you have finished counting to ten.
2. Shout, "I am coming to find you!"
3. Find the friends who are hiding.

Both of the algorithms above use an input to tell the players when they should start following the instructions.

Look at the algorithm for hiding.

The players wait until they hear the finder start to count, then they follow the rest of the instructions.

Hearing someone counting is the input in the algorithm.

Questions

1. What input is used to control the finder?

1 Computational thinking and programming

2 When will Arun start following the instructions in the following algorithm?

> 1 Start when I hear my alarm clock.
> 2 Get out of bed.
> 3 Go and eat my breakfast.

I use an input in my algorithm for getting up.

Adding an input

You can add an input to algorithms that you have already written.

This means that the instructions will only be followed after the input has been given.

I wrote an algorithm to tell someone what to do in a running race. I think I should add an input to the start of the algorithm.

> 1 Run as fast as you can.
> 2 Stop when you get to the finish line.

Question

3 Which would be the best input to start Zara's algorithm?

1.2 Inputs and outputs

Algorithms with different inputs

You can write algorithms that use more than one input.

This means different instructions can be followed when different inputs are given.

Below is an algorithm that uses three inputs.

1. A green card is shown.
2. Draw a cat.
3. A red card is shown.
4. Draw an elephant.
5. A blue card is shown.
6. Draw a lion.

Questions

4. Which part of the algorithm uses a red card as an input?
5. When would someone draw a lion?

Using data as an input

You can also use **data** as an input for an algorithm.

Remember, a piece of data is a fact.

Data that can be used to start algorithms includes time and temperature.

Sofia has written the algorithm below for getting ready for bed.

39

1 Computational thinking and programming

She has used time as an input.

Input:

1

2

3

4

You have used algorithms that use words and algorithms that use pictures.

Which do you find more useful?

Why do you find this type of algorithm more useful?

1.2 Inputs and outputs

> **Did you know?**
>
> Computer systems can automatically open and close windows depending on the temperature.
>
> The windows in this greenhouse open when it is too hot inside.

Algorithms and outputs

We know that output devices share information that has come from the computer.

Output devices include screens, speakers and printers.

Algorithms also have **outputs**.

When you follow an algorithm, the end result is the output.

A recipe for biscuits is an algorithm. The biscuits are the algorithm's output.

Biscuit recipe

Ingredients: butter, sugar, eggs, vanilla, flour, chocolate chips.

Step 1: Mix butter and sugar.

Step 2: Add eggs and vanilla.

Step 3: Add flour and chocolate chips.

Step 4: Mould into biscuits and put on baking tray.

Step 5: Bake in the oven for 10 minutes.

Step 6: Let cool and enjoy!

1 Computational thinking and programming

Unplugged activity 1

Find the output

> You will need:
> a pencil and paper or whiteboard pen and mini whiteboard

Sofia has written an algorithm for drawing a house.

1. Draw a rectangle with the short sides at the top and bottom.
2. Draw a triangle on top of the rectangle.
3. Colour the triangle red.
4. Draw a small rectangle at the bottom and in the centre of the big rectangle.
5. Colour the rectangle green.
6. Draw two squares either side of the small rectangle.
7. Draw two squares above the two squares at the bottom.

Which of the drawings below will be the output of Sofia's algorithm?

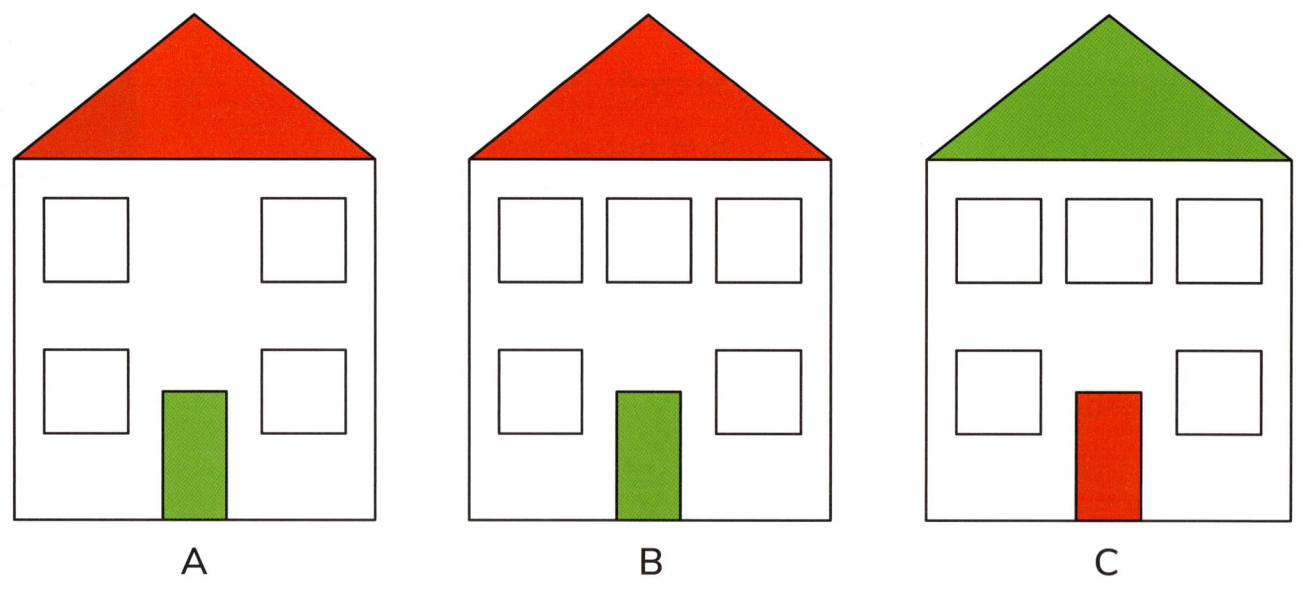

A   B   C

1.2 Inputs and outputs

Using inputs and outputs

When you write an algorithm, you should think about the output you want to get.

You should also think about the inputs you might use to start the algorithm.

Sofia's teacher has asked her to write an algorithm for tidying the classroom.

First, Sofia thinks about the output she wants to get.

The output is a tidy classroom.

Next, Sofia decides that the input will be when the time is 3 p.m.

Here is the algorithm that Sofia wrote.

1. Start when the time is 3 p.m.
2. Put pens and pencils in the table pots.
3. Return reading books to the bookshelf.
4. Pick up any rubbish from the floor and put it in the bin.
5. Place workbooks in the marking box.

1 Computational thinking and programming

Unplugged activity 2

Choosing inputs and outputs

> **You will need:**
> a pencil and paper or whiteboard pen and mini whiteboard

Here are some tasks that you might do every day in your classroom.

Output

Task	Output
Getting ready to go home	You are ready to go home
Getting changed for sports	You are dressed in your sports clothes
Going into school at the start of the day	You go into the classroom
Going for lunch	You eat your lunch

You are going to write an algorithm to help someone complete one of these tasks in your school.

Step 1: Choose one of the tasks above.

Look at the output of the algorithm next to the task.

Step 2: Choose an input for your algorithm.

Think about when you would start doing this task.

44

1.2 Inputs and outputs

Continued

Step 3: Write a set of instructions to show someone else how to complete the task.

In my classroom, we tidy up when our teacher starts the tidy-up timer. My input will be the tidy-up timer starting.

When we go into school at the start of the day, we:
- line up outside
- walk to the cloakroom
- hang up our coats
- go into the classroom.

How am I doing?

Swap your algorithm with a partner. Ask them to give you a tick for each question below they can answer 'yes' to.

- Does the algorithm include a sensible input?
- Does the algorithm have clear instructions?
- Does the algorithm end with the correct output?

Look what I can do!

- ☐ I know that inputs can be used to start algorithms.
- ☐ I can find the inputs in algorithms.
- ☐ I understand what the output of an algorithm is.
- ☐ I can write algorithms that use inputs to create outputs.

1 Computational thinking and programming

> 1.3 Introducing Scratch

We are going to:
- learn how to make simple programs in Scratch
- make changes to programs
- explore how to add more than one character or background to programs
- understand why it is useful to work with other people when we are programming.

Getting started

What do you already know?

- ScratchJr is a programming language.
- You can use command blocks to turn an algorithm into a program in ScratchJr.
- The characters that are controlled by command blocks are called sprites.
- You can run a program in ScratchJr.

backdrop
block palette
bugs
command block
costume
hat blocks
programs
'say' command
Scratch
script area
sprite
stage area
'wait' command

1.3 Introducing Scratch

> **Continued**
>
> **Now try this!**
>
> Think about the last instructions you followed.
>
> - Where did these instructions come from?
> - Were the instructions easy to follow?
> - What happened when you followed the instructions?
>
> Write down the instructions that you followed.
>
> Share them with a partner. Compare your instructions.

Computer programs

In this unit, you will learn how to write computer **programs**.

Computer programs are instructions that a computer can understand.

You have already used ScratchJr to write programs.

Now you will use **Scratch**. Scratch is also a programming language.

Ask your teacher where to find the document called 'Getting started with Scratch'. This document will help you learn how to use Scratch. Work your way through the activities, and then return to this page.

Scratch lets us do a lot more than we did with programs in ScratchJr.

47

1 Computational thinking and programming

Here is an example of a program that has been written using Scratch:

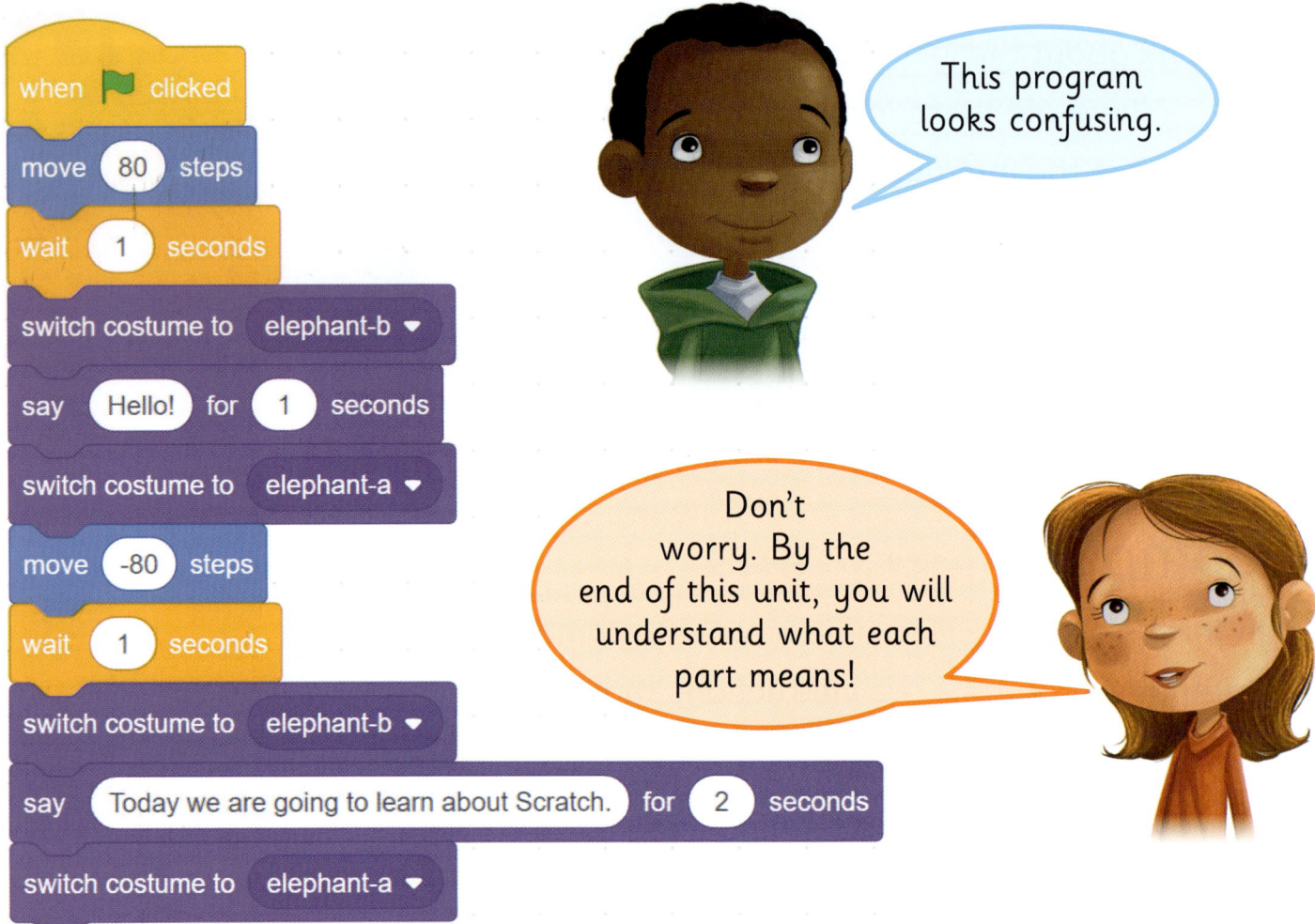

This program looks confusing.

Don't worry. By the end of this unit, you will understand what each part means!

Making programs

In Activity 1 in the 'Getting started with Scratch' document, you ran a program to see what instructions the **command blocks** gave to the computer.

The computer only follows the instructions of the command blocks that are joined together in the **stage area**.

When they are joined together, the command blocks make a program.

1.3 Introducing Scratch

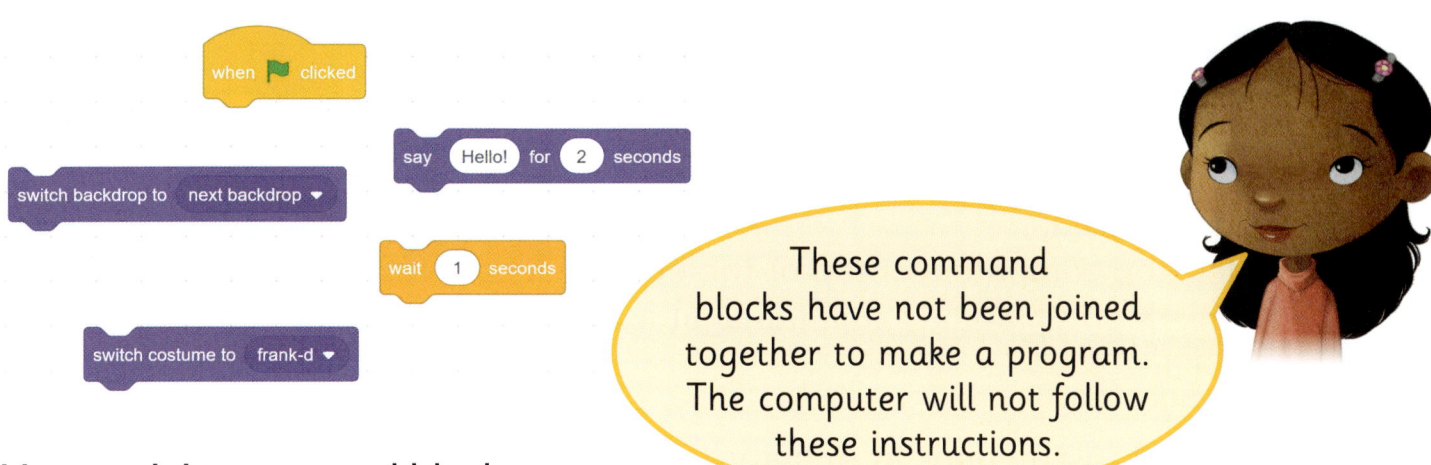

These command blocks have not been joined together to make a program. The computer will not follow these instructions.

You can join command blocks together using your mouse, a touchpad or your finger if you are using a tablet.

Click on a block and drag it underneath the block you want to join it to.

When it is close enough to join, a grey shadow will appear.

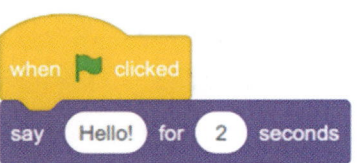

You can now let the block go and it will join the other block.

The block with the green flag on it must be the hat block.

Some blocks are called **hat blocks**.

Hat blocks use inputs. We looked at inputs in Topic 1.2.

Hat blocks tell the computer to start the program when it receives a certain piece of information.

Hat blocks have a round top to show that other blocks can only be joined below them, not above them.

1 Computational thinking and programming

Programming task 1

Joining command blocks

> You will need:
> a desktop computer, laptop or tablet with access to Scratch,
> source file **1.3_joining_command_blocks**

Open Scratch.

Follow the instructions in Activity 1 in the 'Getting started with Scratch' document to open the file your teacher gives you.

The file has some command blocks in the **script area** that need to be joined together to make a program.

Work with a partner to join the blocks together.

Make the program shown below.

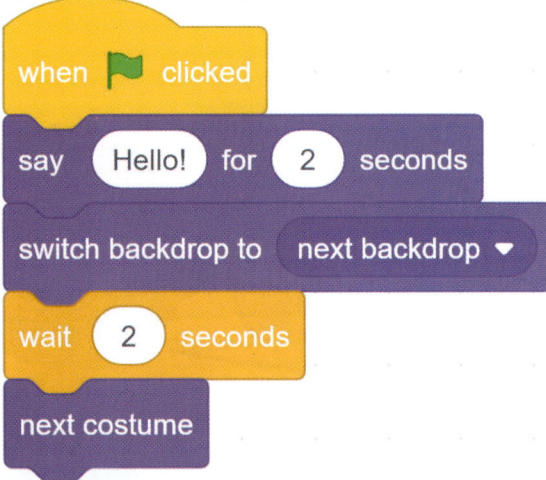

If you join the blocks in the wrong order, you can drag them out of the program and place them back in the script area.

When you have completed the program, run it and say what happens.

Did you know?

You can change the language on the command blocks in Scratch. There are over 70 different languages available.

Reading programs

In this topic, you have made a program in Scratch using wait commands, costume changes and speech bubbles. You have also selected backdrops and sprites for a program.

You are now going to use your knowledge to explain what each command block tells a sprite to do.

Unplugged activity 1

Explaining code

> You will need:
> a pencil and paper or a whiteboard pen and mini whiteboard

Look at this program, which you were shown at the start of this unit.

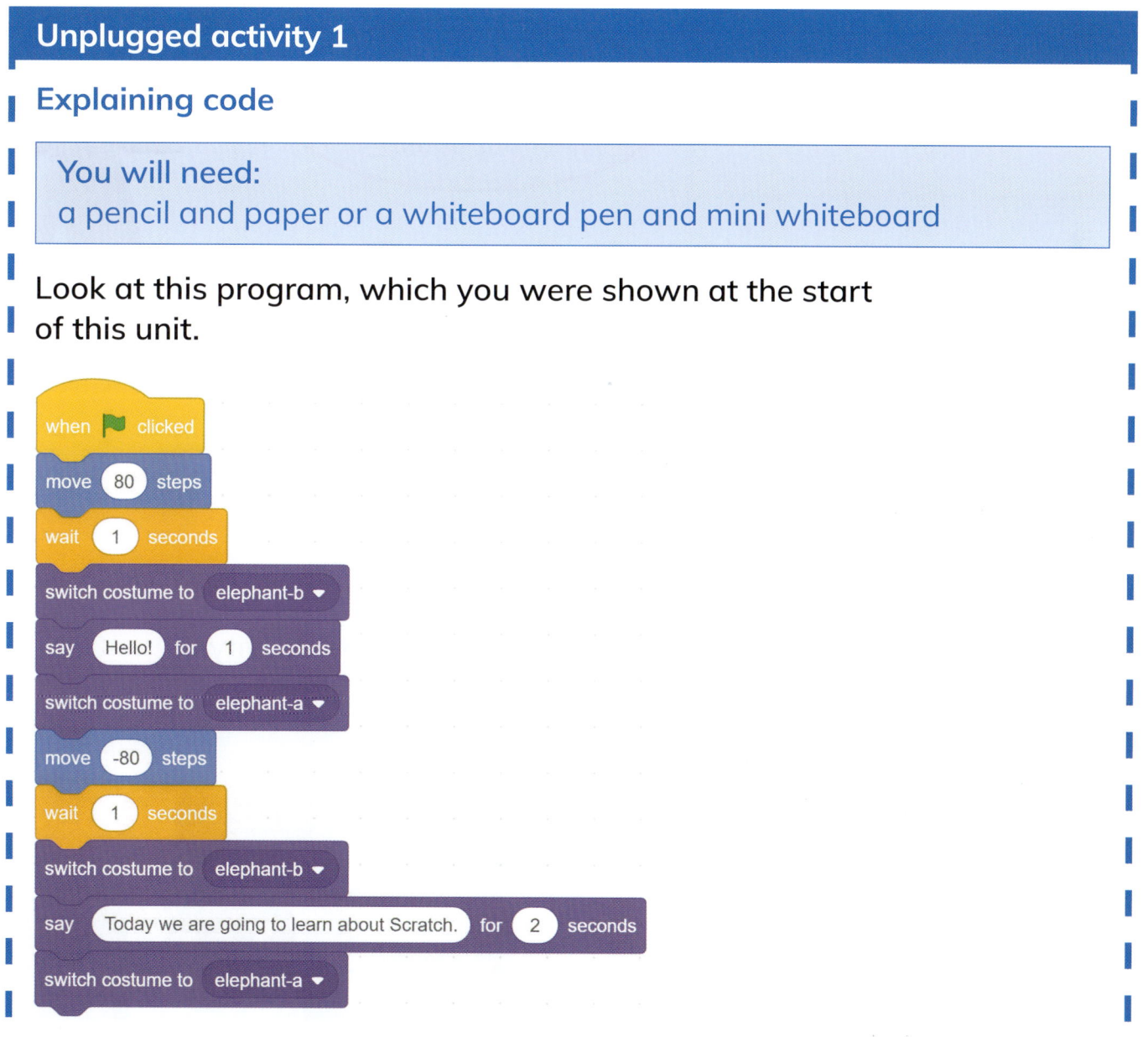

1 Computational thinking and programming

Continued

Discuss with your partner what instruction each command block gives to the **sprite**.

Write down your prediction for each command block in your book.

> The 'move 80 steps' command block makes the sprite move to the right.

This is one of the explanations I wrote in my book.

Working together

In the last activity, you worked with a partner.

Many people think working with another person to write programs is helpful.

This is because one person can write the program and the other person can check for **bugs** (errors).

When people work like this, they switch jobs during the activity.

This means that both people do both jobs.

This is useful because people talk to each other about the program they have made.

They can also discuss different ways to fix any bugs that are in the program.

The next time you work with a partner to write a program, change roles halfway through the activity.

Costume changes

When you dress up, you wear a **costume**.

Sprites in Scratch can also wear costumes.

A costume changes the way that a sprite looks.

It might mean changing a sprite's clothing. Often, it means changing a sprite's position.

Look at this program again:

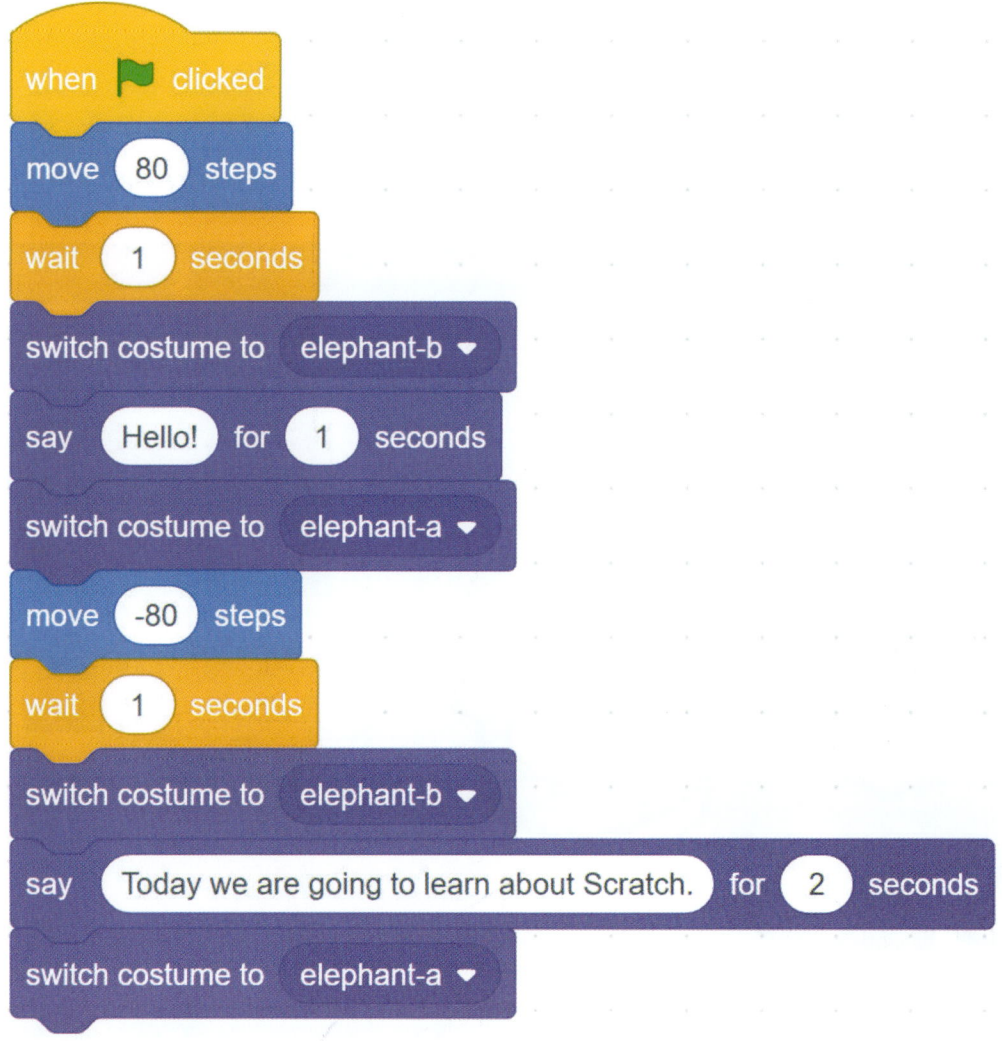

1 Computational thinking and programming

Some of the command blocks in the program tell the computer to change the sprite's costume.

Can you find these blocks?

Some sprites have more than one costume.

Most of the time, the costumes are different body positions.

When you change from one costume to another, you can make the sprite look like it is moving.

To look at a sprite's different costumes, you need to:

- click on the small picture of it underneath the stage area
- then click on the 'Costumes' tab underneath the Scratch logo. It is the second of the three tabs.

The sprite's costumes will be shown on the left-hand side of the screen.

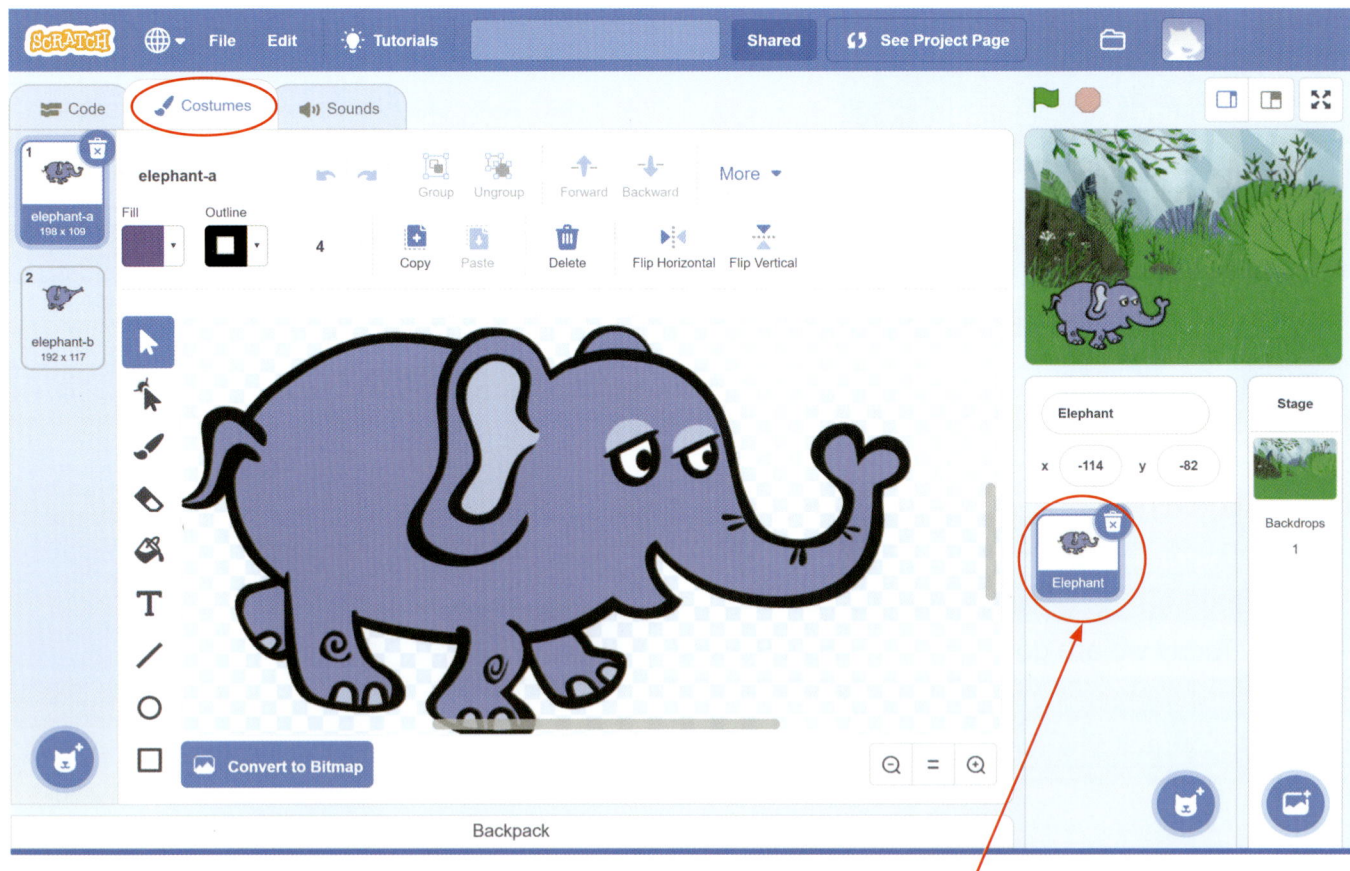

Click this picture to look at a sprite's different costumes.

1.3 Introducing Scratch

Using 'wait' commands

Sometimes, you need to pause the computer program to allow you to see what instructions the sprite is following.

To do this, you need to add a **'wait' command** block.

To find a 'wait' command block, you need to choose the orange 'Control' menu from the **block palette**.

The first command block in the 'Control' menu is the 'wait' command.

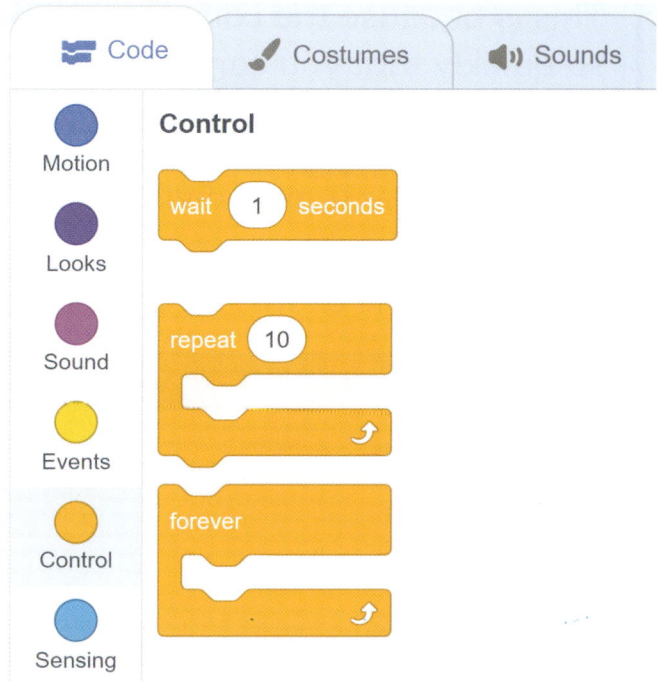

Programming task 2

Adding 'wait' commands

> You will need:
> a desktop computer, laptop or tablet with access to Scratch, source file **1.5_wait_commands**

Open Scratch and open the file your teacher gives you.

Look at the program. How many costumes are used?

Step 1: Run the program by clicking on the green flag above the stage area.

How many different costumes did you see?

Even though the program uses four costumes, you do not see the sprite change its costume.

55

1 Computational thinking and programming

Continued

This is because the computer follows the commands so quickly that you cannot see each costume.

Sofia knows how to solve this problem.

Sofia chooses a 'wait' command block and adds it to the program.

To do this, she drags it from the menu to the script area.

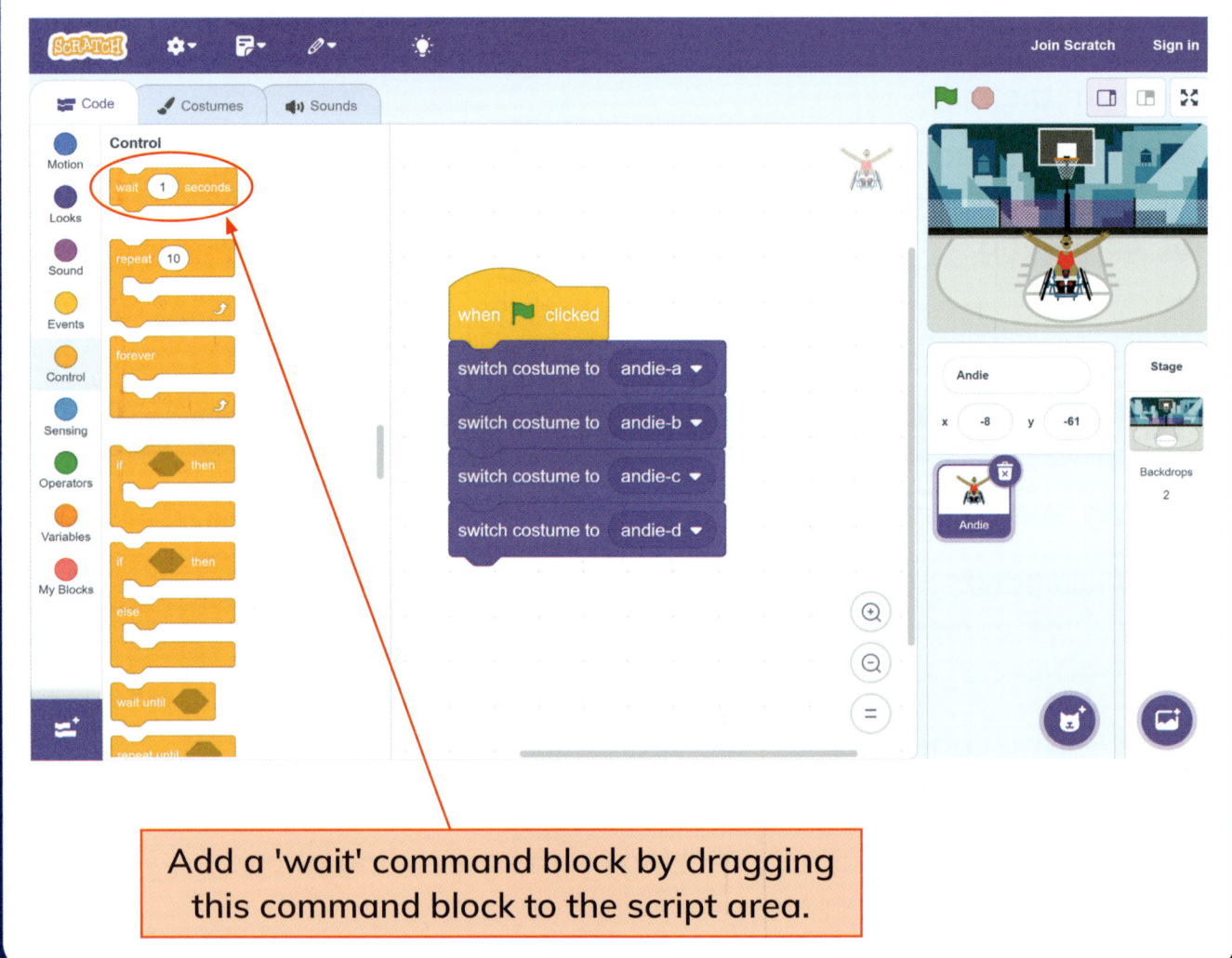

Add a 'wait' command block by dragging this command block to the script area.

56

1.3 Introducing Scratch

Continued

Sofia drags the first 'wait' command block in between the first two purple blocks.

She waits until the grey shadow appears, then lets it go.

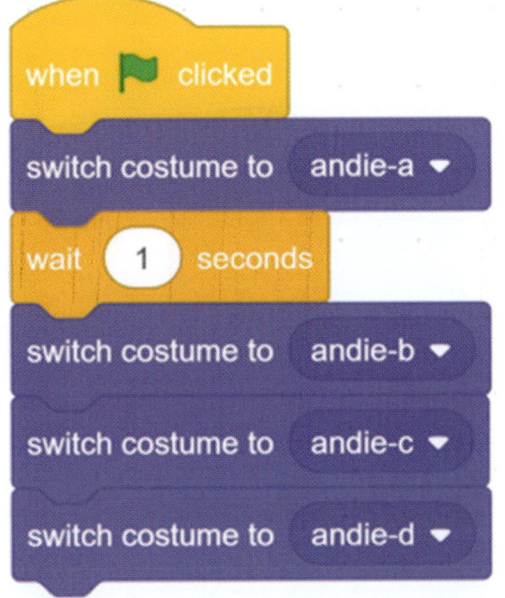

This time I saw two different costumes.

Sofia runs the program again by clicking on the green flag above the stage area.

What happens this time?

Step 2: Work with a partner to add two more 'wait' commands so that each of the sprite's costumes can be seen.

Remember to:

- change jobs with your partner halfway through the activity
- discuss what you are doing.

Step 3: Save your program.

To do this, go to 'File' and 'Save to your computer'.

Now you are going to use some of the things you have learnt about Scratch to write a program.

1 Computational thinking and programming

Programming task 3

Making a program

> **You will need:**
> a desktop computer, laptop or tablet with access to Scratch

Arun has made a plan for a program he wants to write.

- Start: when the green flag is clicked
- Backdrop: castle
- Sprite: dragon
- Costumes: three costumes, which change every second

Work with a partner to write a program in Scratch that matches Arun's plan.

You will need to open Scratch and choose 'Create' to start a new file.

Remember that one of you should write the program and one of you should check for bugs.

Do not forget to swap jobs halfway through.

When you have finished, save your program.

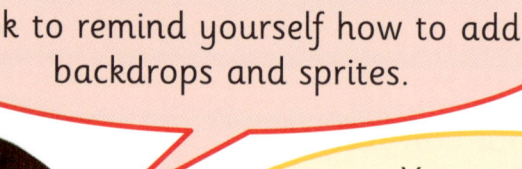

You can look back in this book to remind yourself how to add backdrops and sprites.

You can use the colour of the block to work out which menu it is in. The 'change costume' block is purple. It can be found in the 'Looks' menu.

1.3 Introducing Scratch

> **Continued**
>
> **How am I doing?**
>
> Look at the sentences below and choose the one that best describes you.
> - I felt confident completing this activity.
> - I needed help from my partner with this activity.
> - I was unsure about this activity.
>
> Discuss with a partner why you chose that sentence.

In this activity, you checked the program your partner wrote. How did you use your learning when you did this?

How does programming with a partner help you to learn?

1 Computational thinking and programming

Say something

Look at the program from the start of the topic again:

The elephant uses speech bubbles to speak. You are going to learn about this command block.

Questions

1 Which command blocks give the instruction to show words in speech bubbles?

2 Which menu will you find these command blocks in? (Look at the colour of the command blocks.)

1.3 Introducing Scratch

A **'say' command** block adds a speech bubble to a sprite. There are two pieces of information we can change in the 'say' command block:

- We can change the words that the sprite says.
- We can change how long the speech bubble stays on the screen. This will give people enough time to read it.

Activity 1

Who am I?

> You will need:
> a desktop computer, laptop or tablet with access to Scratch, source file **1.6_who_am_I**, a pencil and paper or whiteboard pen and mini whiteboard

You are going to add some information to Scratch to describe this sprite:

Work with a partner. Copy the table and choose some details to describe your sprite.

Sprite's name	
Sprite's favourite colour	
Sprite's favourite lesson	
Sprite's favourite sport	

Open Scratch and open the file your teacher gives you.

Now use the information in your table.

Step 1: Click your pointer next to the words that are already in each 'say' command block to add information to them.

Step 2: You should also click on the number of seconds that each speech bubble stays on the screen and change it.

1 Computational thinking and programming

On the move

Let's look at a different command in our program:

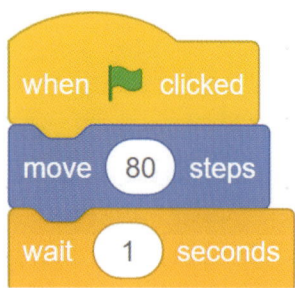

The blue blocks make the sprite move.

They are found in the 'Motion' menu.

You are going to use one of these blocks and change the information in it to make the sprite move different amounts and in two different directions.

> **Programming task 4**
>
> **Investigating steps**
>
>
>
> **You will need:**
> a desktop computer, laptop or tablet with access to Scratch
>
> Copy the table below into your notebook.
>
> | Moves right a short way | Moves right a long way | Moves left a short way | Moves left a long way |
> |---|---|---|---|
> | | | | |

62

1.3 Introducing Scratch

Continued

Work with a partner. Open Scratch and create a new file.

Step 1: Delete the cat sprite and add a sprite of your choice.

Step 2: Now write the program below.

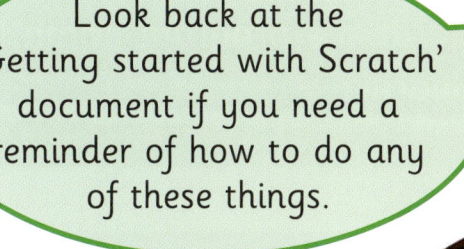
Look back at the 'Getting started with Scratch' document if you need a reminder of how to do any of these things.

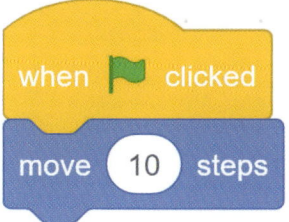

My sprite moved a short way to the right. I am going to write 'move 10 steps' in that column of the table.

Step 3: When you have written the program, run it.

What did the sprite do?

Decide which part of the table to write the command in.

Step 4: Next, change the steps so that the sprite follows each of the programs below.

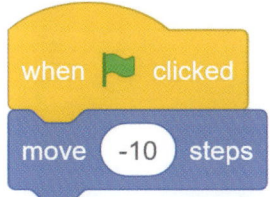 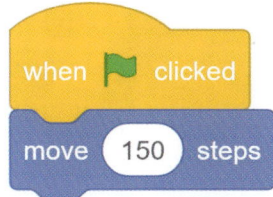 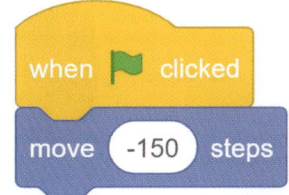

Step 5: Run each program and place the information in the correct column in the table.

Now you know how to move a sprite left and right.

Look closely. Some of the numbers have a minus symbol (−) before them. This makes the sprite move to the left.

1 Computational thinking and programming

You were shown a computer program at the start of this topic.
You looked at the same program again at the end of the topic.
Has looking at the program again helped you to see how much you have learnt?

Look what I can do!

- ☐ I can make simple programs in Scratch.
- ☐ I can make changes to programs.
- ☐ I can add more than one sprite or backdrop to programs.
- ☐ I know why it is useful to work with another person when I am programming.

1.4 Moving and changing sprites

We are going to:

- use programs that control two sprites (characters)
- explain which piece of code is for which sprite
- make changes to a program
- add command blocks to return sprites to how they were at the start
- understand why making a mistake can be helpful.

command block script area
costume sprite
initialisation stage area
program 'wait' command
Scratch

Getting started

What do you already know?

- How to make programs in Scratch.
- How to add more than one sprite to programs.
- How to change how long a speech bubble stays on the screen.

65

1 Computational thinking and programming

> **Continued**
>
> **Now try this!**
>
> > You will need:
> > a desktop computer, laptop or tablet with access to Scratch, source file **1.7_changing_program**
>
> You learnt about Scratch in the last topic. Now you are going to quickly remind yourself how to use it.
>
> Work with a partner.
>
> Open Scratch and open the file your teacher gives you.
>
> Change the program so that the sprite:
>
> - moves further to the right
> - pauses for less time
> - uses more than two costumes
> - says what its name is (you can make up its name).

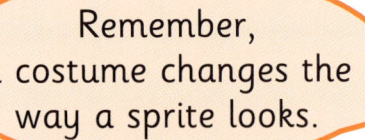

Remember, a costume changes the way a sprite looks.

Two sprites

In the previous topic, all the programs had one sprite.

In this topic, you are going to write programs with two sprites.

When you have two sprites, they can talk to each other!

You will use lots of the command blocks that you used in the previous topic.

1.4 Moving and changing sprites

> **Activity 1**
>
> **Two sprites and two pieces of code**
>
> > You will need:
> > a desktop computer or laptop with access to Scratch,
> > source file **1.8_two_sprites**
>
> Open Scratch and open the file your teacher gives you.
>
> This file has two sprites.
>
> Each sprite has its own piece of code.
>
>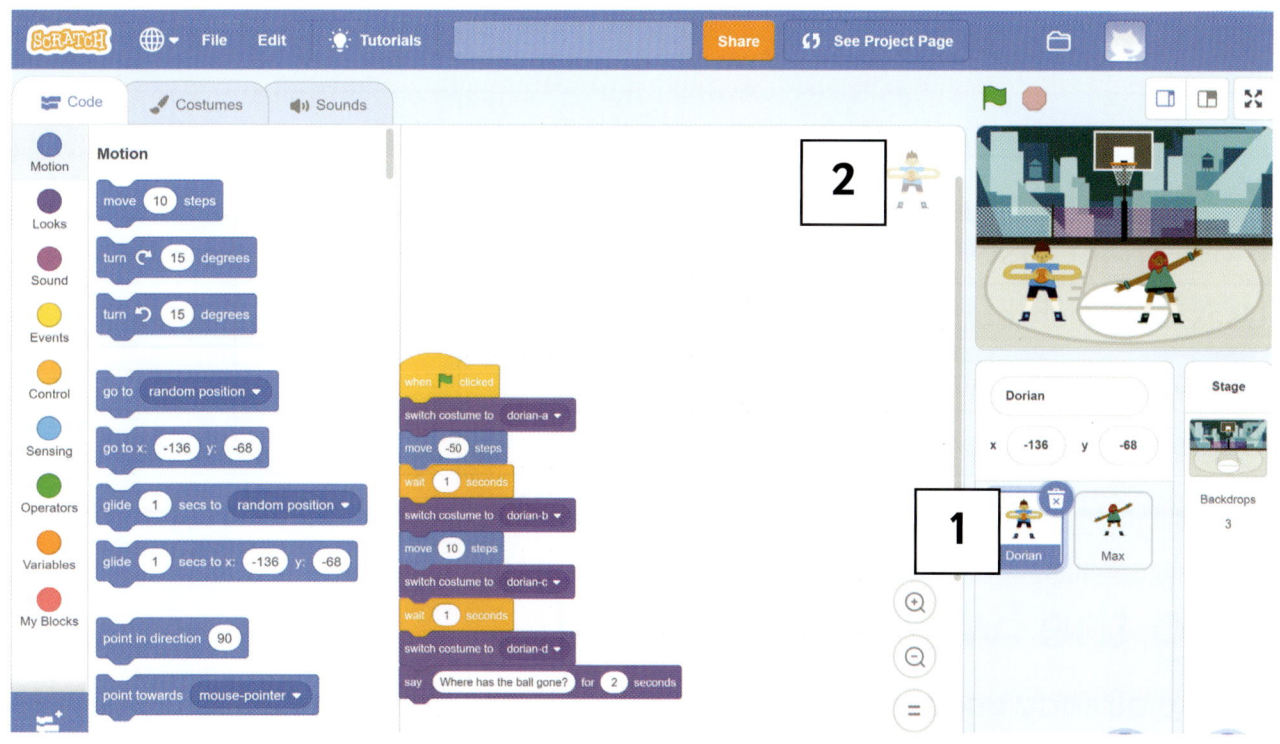
>
> **Step 1:** To see each sprite's piece of code, click on the little picture of the sprite below the stage area.
>
> **Step 2:** To help you remember which sprite's code you are looking at, a little picture of the sprite is shown at the top right corner of the script area.

67

1 Computational thinking and programming

> **Continued**
>
> Copy the table below.
>
> Work with a partner to look at the pieces of code for each sprite.
>
> *Remember, there will be a minus (−) symbol to show that a sprite is moving left.*
>
> You can see the sprite's names underneath their pictures.
>
> Decide if each description is about Dorian's code, Max's code or both pieces of code. You do not need to run the code to complete this activity.
>
> Tick the right answers.
>
> | | Dorian | Max | Both |
> |---|---|---|---|
> | Moves left first | | | |
> | Moves right first | | | |
> | Uses a speech bubble to talk | | | |
> | Has two 'wait' commands | | | |
> | Changes costume four times | | | |

Using the 'wait' command

You have already used the 'wait' command block in the previous topic.

This pauses the sprite before it follows the next instruction.

The 'wait' command block is also useful when we are writing programs for more than one sprite.

We can pause one sprite while the other sprite is doing an action or talking.

It is how we can make it look like the sprites are talking to each other.

1.4 Moving and changing sprites

Each time one of your sprites speaks, the other sprite will need a 'wait' command block for the same amount of time.

Initialisation

Sometimes after running a program, you need to drag the sprites back to the start so that you can run the program again.

You can add a command block that moves the sprites back to the start, or changes them back to how they looked at the start.

This is a bit like playing a board game where the pieces and cards have to be moved back to the start before you can play the game again.

This means that you do not have to move the sprites back yourself.

This is called **initialisation**.

> **Programming task 1**
>
> **Animal race**
>
> > You will need:
> > a desktop computer, laptop or tablet with access to Scratch, source file **1.9_animal_race**
>
> Open Scratch and open the file your teacher gives you.
>
> Run the program. You should see two animals race across the screen.
>
> Click on the little picture of each sprite below the stage area to look at the code that gives each sprite their instructions.
>
> Follow these instructions to add a command block to each piece of code so that the characters move back to the start before they begin the race.

1 Computational thinking and programming

Continued

Step 3: Click on the 'Motion' menu.

Step 1: Drag each sprite back to the place where it started. Then look at the sprite's information below the stage area.

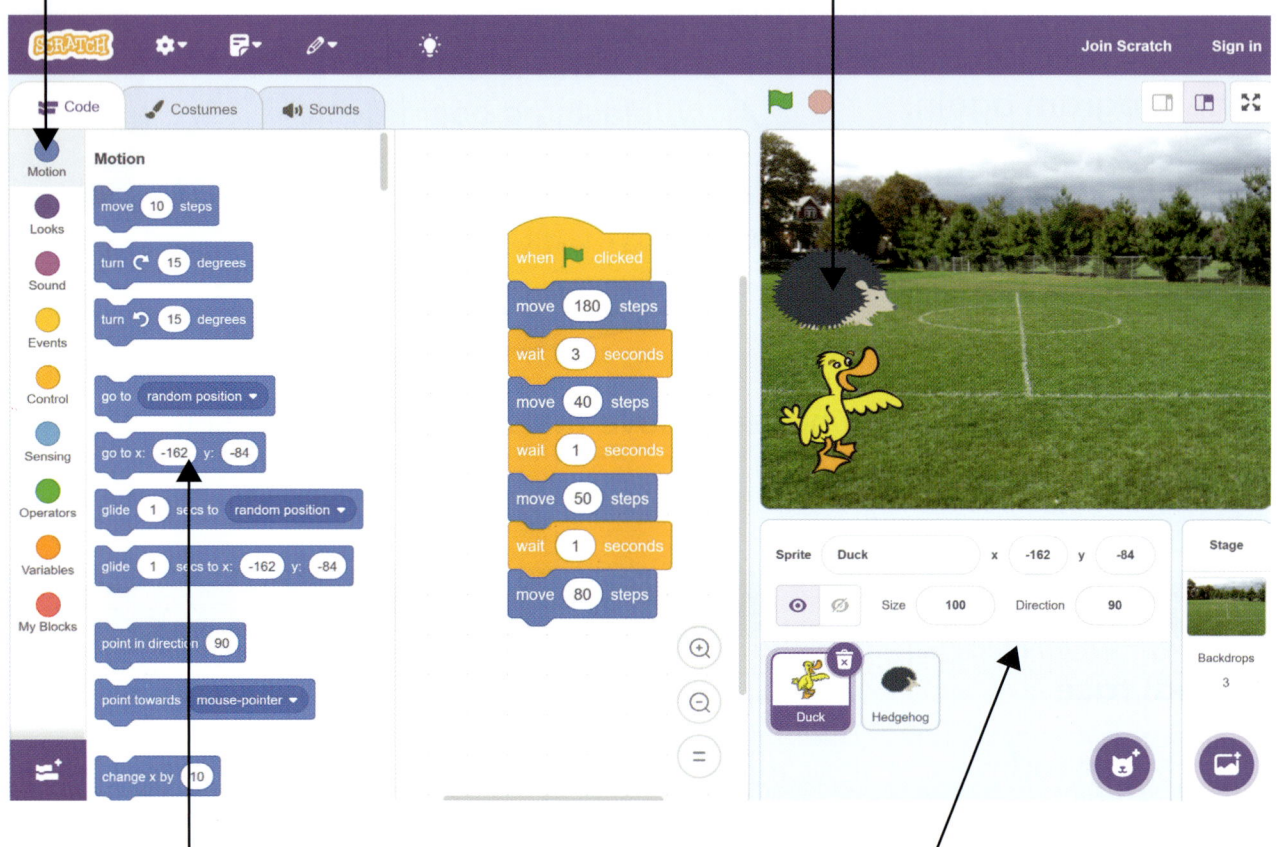

Step 4: The 'go to' command block gives instructions to the sprite about where to go. The two numbers in the command block will be the same as the two numbers in the sprite's information bar that give its position.

Step 2: The information bar below the stage area tells you about the sprite's position (place).

This information is the numbers next to the letters x and y. The computer uses these two numbers to work out where the sprite should be placed.

70

1.4 Moving and changing sprites

Continued

Step 5: Drag the 'go to' command and place it under the hat block that starts the piece of code.

This instruction will put the sprite in this place when the program is started.

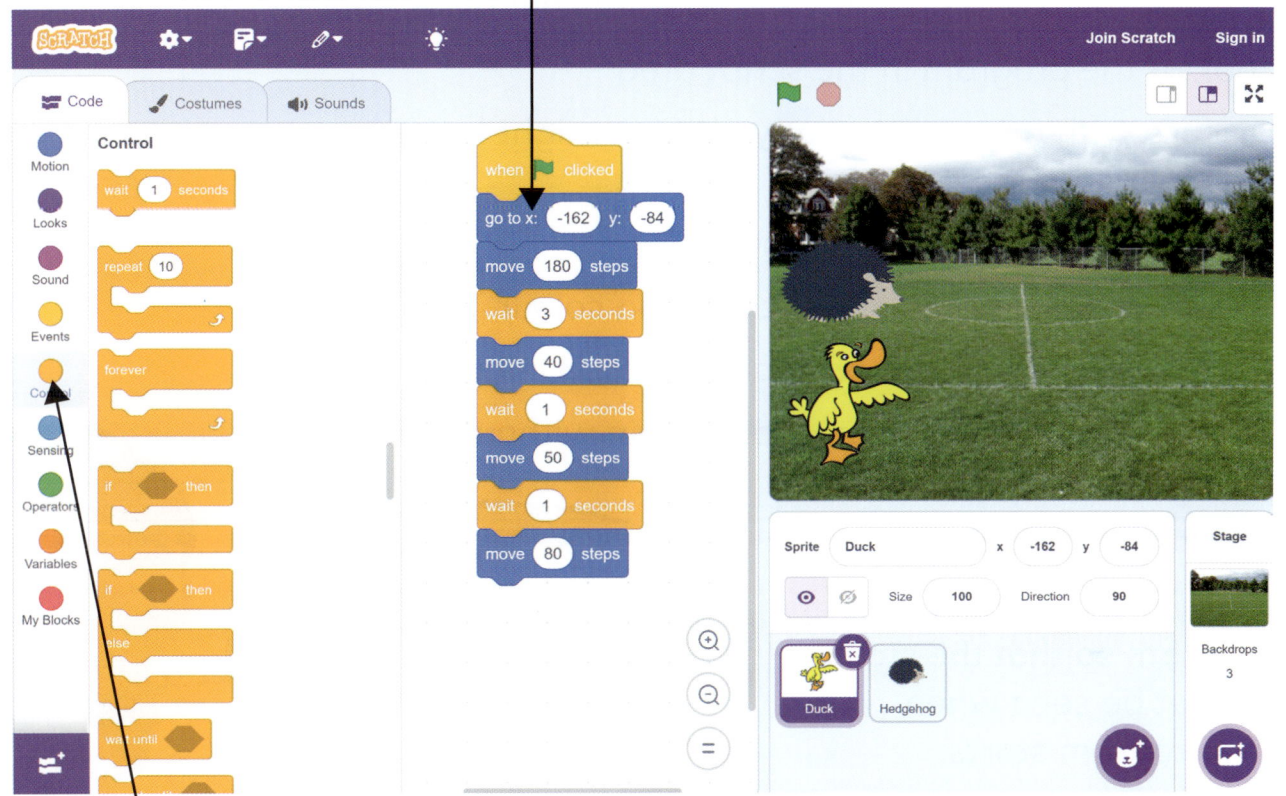

Step 6: Look at the 'Control' menu. Drag a 'wait' command block to the program under the 'go to' block you have just added.

This block will allow you to see that the sprite has returned to its original position.

Step 7: Repeat these steps for the other sprite, then run your program. The animals should race just like the first time.

Run your program again.

The animals will go back to the start before racing again.

71

1   Computational thinking and programming

Programming task 2

A colourful star

> **You will need:**
> a desktop computer, laptop or tablet with access to Scratch, source file **1.10_colourful_star**

Open Scratch and open the file your teacher gives you.

Look at the program in the script area.

Discuss with a partner what you think might happen when you run the program.

Run the program. What happened?

You should have seen a star changing colour.

It would be good if this program included initialisation.

Then you could run the program again without having to change its costume.

Work with a partner.

Help Zara to initialise the program so that the star cannot be seen when the program starts.

When I run the program for a second time the star is already visible. It does not return to being black.

You should look at the sprite's costumes to decide which one it should start with.

1.4 Moving and changing sprites

Continued

You will need to add another 'switch costume' block.

Remember to add a 'wait' command block before it.

If you want to see all the different costumes, you can click on the Costumes tab, next to the Code tab.

> Remember, the colour of the command block tells you which menu to use.

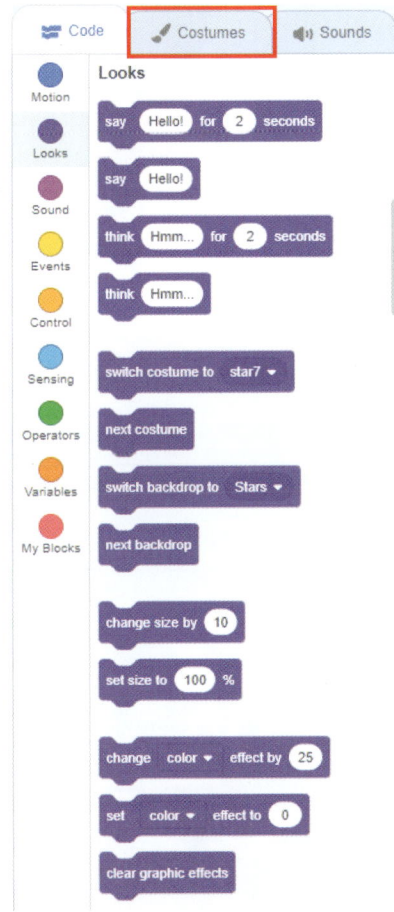

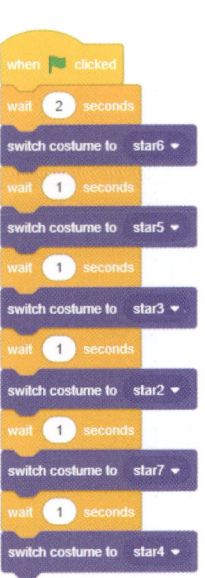

How are we doing?

Did you know where to look to find information about the sprite's costumes?

1 Computational thinking and programming

Learning from mistakes

People often make mistakes in computing.

Sometimes, this is because they are trying to find new ways to do things.

When people work together to write programs, they can help each other to fix problems.

One person might have already made the same mistake and fixed it in another program.

When you fix a mistake, you should try not to make that mistake again.

But if you do, you will already know how to fix the mistake.

This is because you have learnt from your mistake.

> I tried to do Programming task 2, but I made a mistake in initialisation. The next time I write a program, I will check that part of the program carefully.

Did you know?

In 1997, a chess expert called Garry Kasparov was beaten by a chess computer.

But the computer's winning move was actually a mistake. It was a bug in the software!

What mistakes have you made when you have been programming with Scratch?

What have you learnt from making these mistakes?

1.4 Moving and changing sprites

Programming task 3

Underwater initialisation

> You will need:
> a desktop computer, laptop or tablet with access to Scratch, source file **1.11_underwater**

Open Scratch and open the file your teacher gives you.

It has an underwater scene and a fish sprite which has different costumes.

Work with a partner to write a program that uses initialisation, moves the fish to different fixed positions and changes its costume.

You should also use 'wait' commands to let people see the costume change before the fish moves again.

All of the command blocks that you need for this program have already been placed in the script area.

You need to join the blocks to make a program.

Remember to test your program!

If you find any mistakes, use the mistakes to help you understand what to change or what to do differently next time.

Look what I can do!

- [ ] I can understand programs that control two sprites and have two pieces of code running at the same time.
- [ ] I can make changes to a program.
- [ ] I can add command blocks to programs to return sprites to how they were at the start.
- [ ] I understand how mistakes in computing can be helpful.

1 Computational thinking and programming

> 1.5 Clear and concise programs

We are going to:

- understand why writing clear and concise programs is useful
- learn how to write clear and concise programs
- find out how to combine command blocks
- learn how to remove unused command blocks.

backdrop
combine
command block
concise
costume
program
Scratch
script area
sprite
stage area

Getting started

What do you already know?

- How to write programs in Scratch.
- That repeat instructions can make algorithms shorter.

1.5 Clear and concise programs

Continued

Now try this!

Sofia is marking her partner's spelling test.

She is using the algorithm below to help her to do this.

1. Look at the word.
2. Check if the word has been spelt correctly by looking at the spelling list.
3. Place a tick next to the word if it has been spelt correctly.
4. Add up the number of ticks.
5. Write down this number.
6. Give the test back to your partner.

Sofia will repeat some of the instructions in the algorithm.

Write out the algorithm.

Then highlight any steps that will be done more than once.

1 Computational thinking and programming

Combining command blocks

You have already learnt that algorithms should be concise.

When you write concise algorithms, you do not use unnecessary words.

That means you do not use extra words that are not needed.

You should also make your computer programs clear and concise.

Unnecessary words make algorithms harder to follow.

It is difficult to debug (find and fix errors) programs that are not clear and concise.

When you write a program with your partner, the person checking the program should check if it is clear and concise.

One way of making your programs clear and concise is to see if the same command block is used several times.

If it is, you might be able to **combine** the command blocks.

Combine means you put two or more command blocks together to make one command block. This single command block gives the same instruction as the command blocks you have combined.

1.5 Clear and concise programs

This is a program that Arun has written.
He wants to move a sprite 50 steps.

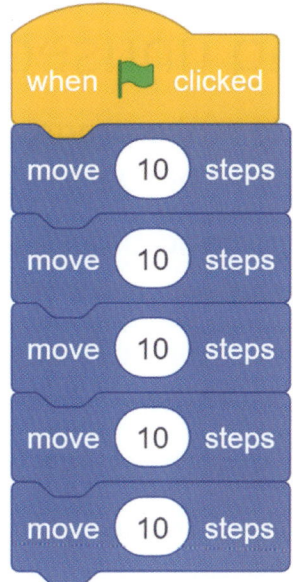

Sofia thinks that some of Arun's command blocks can be combined to make the program clear and concise.

Arun rewrites his program.

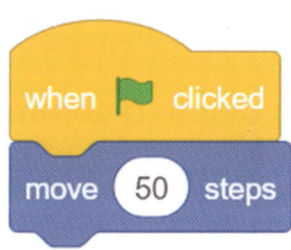

Questions

1. Which command blocks has Arun combined?
2. Which instruction has Arun used instead?
3. Will the sprite still move the same number of steps?

When you write clear and concise programs, they are easier to debug. This is because there are fewer command blocks to check.

Are there any other ways to write clear and concise programs?

1 Computational thinking and programming

Removing unused commands

Another way to make programs clear and concise is to remove command blocks that are not being used.

In Scratch, command blocks that are not joined can stay in the script area.

These blocks are not part of the program because they are not joined to anything.

The computer ignores these instructions.

If you do not need these instructions, they should be deleted.

Removing unused blocks makes it easier to check your program.

This is because you are not distracted by the unused blocks.

To delete a command block that you no longer need:

1 Drag the block back to the block palette.
2 When you let go of the block, it will be deleted.

If you are not sure how to do this, ask a partner or your teacher for help.

1.5 Clear and concise programs

> **Programming task 1**
>
> **Playing baseball**
>
> > **You will need:**
> > a desktop computer, laptop or tablet with access to Scratch, source file **1.12_playing_baseball**
>
> Open Scratch and open the file your teacher gives you.
>
> The program contains two pieces of code that are used to control two sprites.
>
> Work with a partner.
>
> **Step 1:** Run the program to find out what happens.
>
> Remember, press the green flag above the stage area to do this.
>
>
>
> In 'Pitcher's' code, there are some unused command blocks in the script area.
>
> You can choose one of them to finish the piece of code.
>
> **Step 2:** Connect it to the other command blocks. Then delete the other two blocks.
>
> **Step 3:** There are also some command blocks in 'Pitcher's' code that can be combined.
>
> Find these blocks and combine them.
>
> **Step 4:** Then delete the blocks that you no longer need.

1 Computational thinking and programming

Writing a clear and concise program

You have learnt how to do a lot of different things in Scratch over the last three topics.

You are now going to use lots of the things that you have learnt to write a program.

You will work with a partner.

Remember, working with someone else to write a program helps you:

- look for errors
- learn from mistakes you have both made before
- remind each other how to write a clear and concise program.

Programming task 2

A clear and concise program

You will need:
a desktop computer, laptop or tablet with access to Scratch

Marcus has made a plan for a program he is trying to make.

What will the program look like?

- Backdrop: Jurassic
- Sprite: Dinosaur2 (red triceratops)

How will the program start?

- Place: bottom left of the screen
- Costume: dinosaur2-a

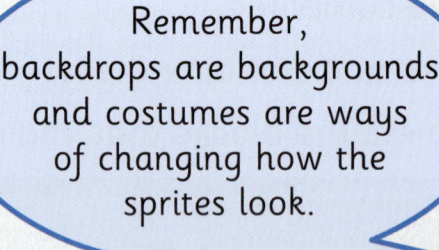

Remember, backdrops are backgrounds and costumes are ways of changing how the sprites look.

1.5 Clear and concise programs

> **Continued**
>
> **What will the program do?**
> - Wait for 1 second.
> - Move right 100 steps.
> - Change costume to dinosaur2-d.
> - Wait for 1 second.
> - Move right 100 steps.
> - Change costume to dinosaur2-c.

You are going to work with a partner to turn Marcus's plan into a program.

Before you start, think about how you will:

- add a backdrop
- add a new sprite
- initialise the sprite
- keep the program clear and concise.

Open Scratch and make a new file.

Work with your partner to write a program using Marcus's plan.

Remember to delete any unused command blocks.

What could you do if you have forgotten how to do any of these things?

You could ask someone else in your class to explain how they are going to do it.

You could look back at the previous pages in this book.

1 Computational thinking and programming

Continued

How are we doing?

Show your program to another pair.

Ask them to use the checklist below to see if you have written a clear and concise program.

You should check their program using the checklist too.

- Could any command blocks be combined?
- Do any command blocks need to be removed from the program?
- Have all unused command blocks been deleted?
- Does the program do what Marcus's plan says it should do?

Did the other pair write a clear and concise program?

If they did, tell them.

If they did not, tell them how they can make it clear and concise. Use the checklist to help you.

Writing clear and concise programs is useful.
They are easier to debug because they are well organised.
How can being well organised help you to learn?

Look what I can do!

- ☐ I can write clear and concise programs.
- ☐ I can combine command blocks.
- ☐ I can remove unused command blocks.

> 1.6 Introducing the micro:bit

We are going to:

- find out that the BBC micro:bit can be programmed to turn lights on and off
- learn how to write programs that control the micro:bit's lights
- download and transfer a program to a micro:bit
- explore some of the micro:bit's input devices
- write a program that uses the micro:bit's input devices
- test and debug programs.

command blocks
debug
download
import
input
LEDs

micro:bit
off-screen
output
program
simulator
toolbox

Getting started

What do you already know?

- Inputs can be used to start an algorithm.
- An output is what happens when an algorithm is followed.
- How to write a program in Scratch to control a character (sprite).

1 Computational thinking and programming

Continued

Now try this!

Look at the algorithm below. It gives instructions for how to draw a creature.

1 Draw a square body.
2 Add three legs to the body.
3 Add a long, twisty tail.
4 Draw a triangle-shaped head on top of the body.
5 Give the creature two floppy ears.
6 Add two circles for its eyes.

Now look at the three drawings of creatures below.

Which one would be the output of the algorithm above?

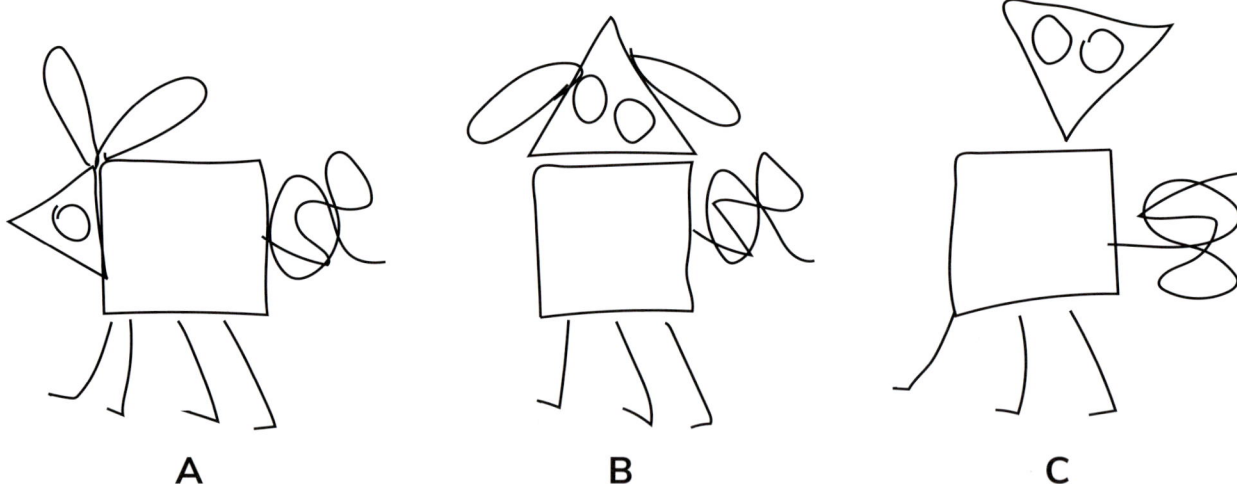

A B C

Explain why you chose the creature you did and why you did not choose the other two.

1.6 Introducing the micro:bit

On-screen and off-screen

Earlier in this unit, you wrote programs using Scratch.

The instructions in your code were followed on the screen by the sprites.

This was the output of your code.

Sometimes, people write computer programs where the instructions are followed off-screen.

This means not on a screen.

These can include:

- turning lights on and off
- making robots move
- controlling traffic lights.

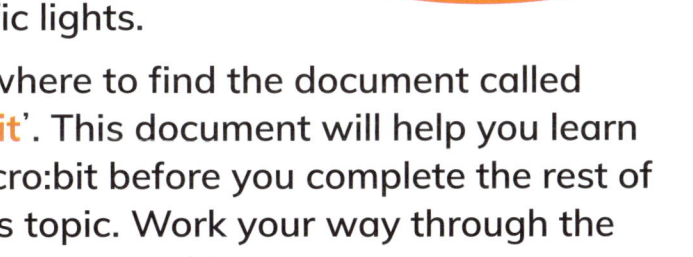

The commands you wrote for the Bee-Bot were followed off-screen.

Ask your teacher where to find the document called 'Using the micro:bit'. This document will help you learn how to use the micro:bit before you complete the rest of the activities in this topic. Work your way through the activities and then return to this page.

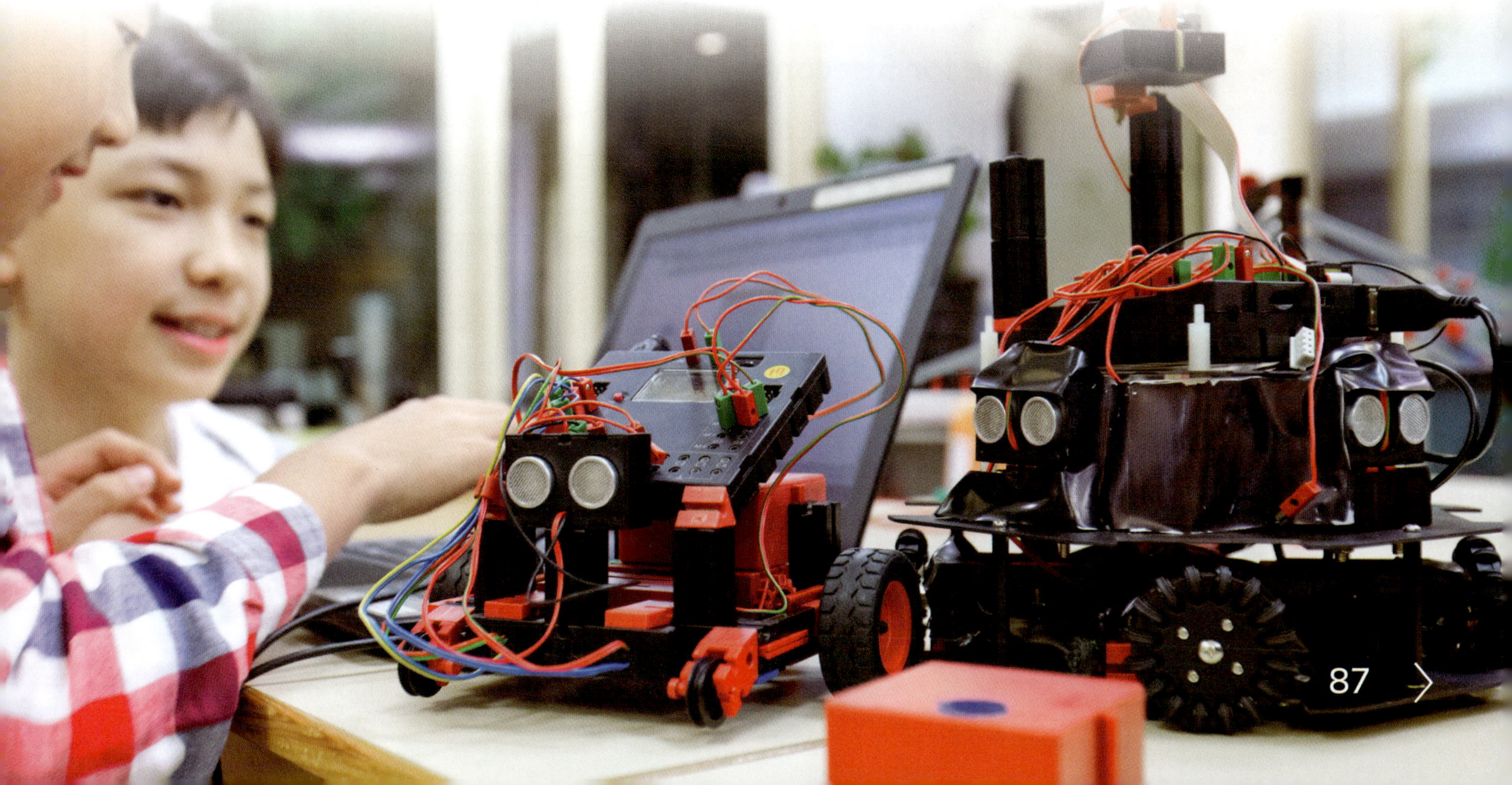

1 Computational thinking and programming

> **Did you know?**
>
> There are lots of fun things you can do with a micro:bit.
>
> You can use it to count the number of steps you take.
>
> The micro:bit can be used as a compass to tell you which direction you are facing.
>
> It can even be programmed to play music!

Programming task 1

Showing shapes

> **You will need:**
> a desktop computer or laptop, a micro:bit, a micro USB B cable and access to the MakeCode website; or a tablet, a micro:bit, a battery pack and access to the MakeCode app, source file **1.14_showing_shapes**

Arun wants to show some shapes using the micro:bit.

- Show a square for 5 seconds.
- Show a triangle for 5 seconds.
- Show a diamond for 5 seconds.
- Turn all the **LEDs** off.

I have written an algorithm to help me write my program.

Go to the MakeCode website.

You are going to **import** a file that your teacher gives you.

Import means to copy or move something from one place to another.

1.6 Introducing the micro:bit

Continued

Step 1: Click on the 'Import' button.

Step 2: Choose 'Import File...'

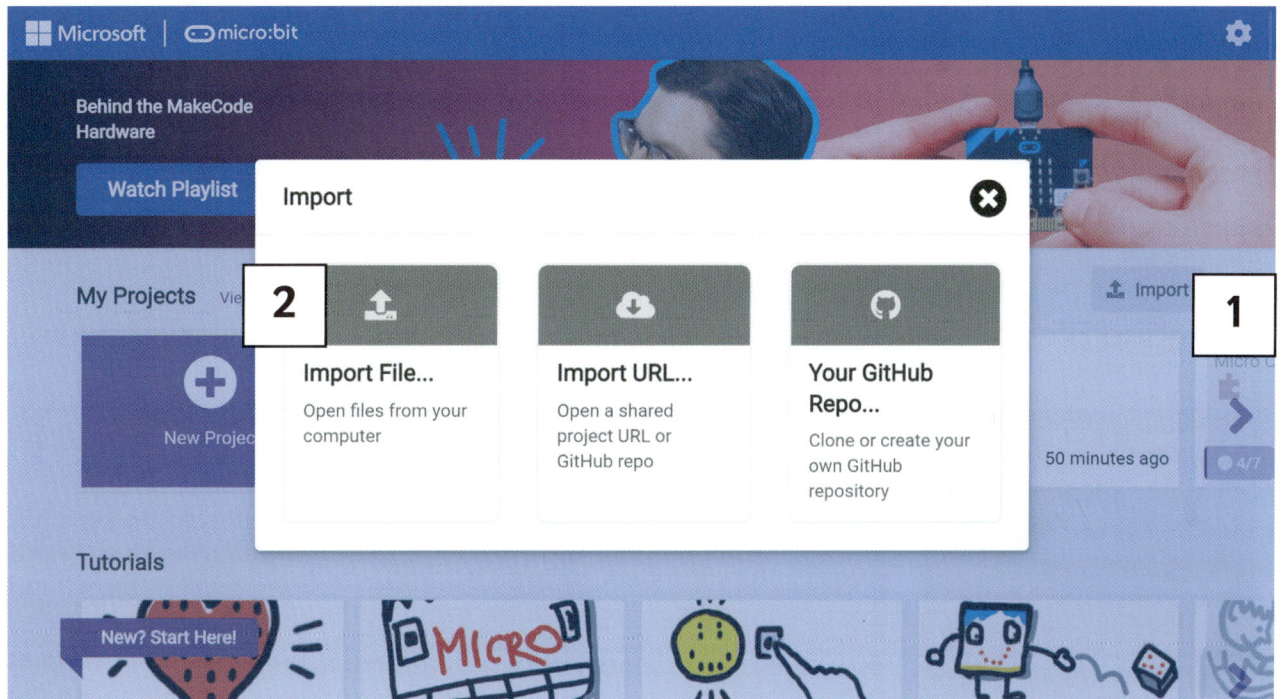

Now you can find the file. Your teacher will tell you where the file is saved.

Step 3: To upload the file from your computer to MakeCode, click on 'Go ahead!'

1 Computational thinking and programming

> **Continued**
>
> When the file has been uploaded, the programming page will open and you will be able to see the program.
>
> Arun has chosen the command blocks that he needs to use for his program.
>
> He has not chosen which LEDs need to be turned on for each picture.
>
> Select which LEDs are needed to show each shape Arun picked.
>
> Arun has not changed the number of seconds in the pause command block.
>
>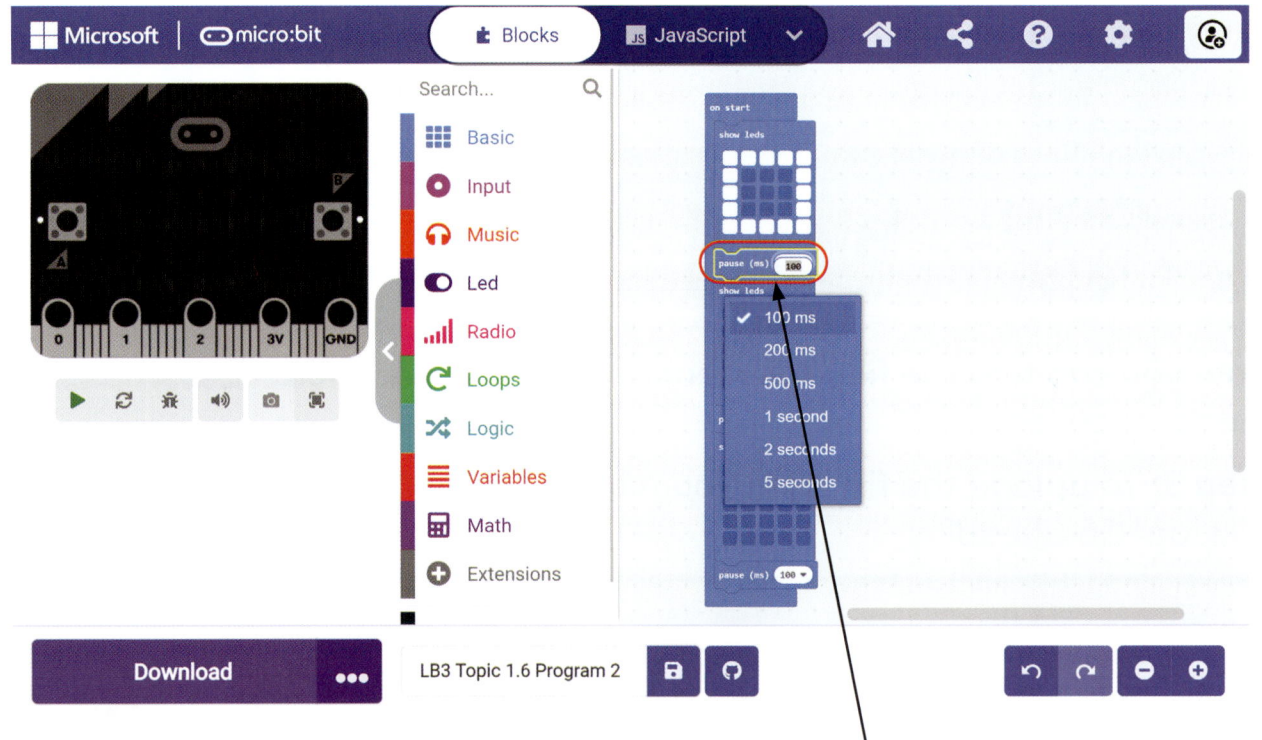
>
> **Step 4:** Click on the arrow next to the number 100 in the pause command block. A menu will appear. You should select five seconds from this menu. The pause command block will then show the number 5000. This means 5000 milliseconds, which is the same as five seconds. Repeat this for the other two pause command blocks.

1.6 Introducing the micro:bit

Continued

Arun has not turned off all the LEDs at the end of his program. You will need to add another command block to do this.

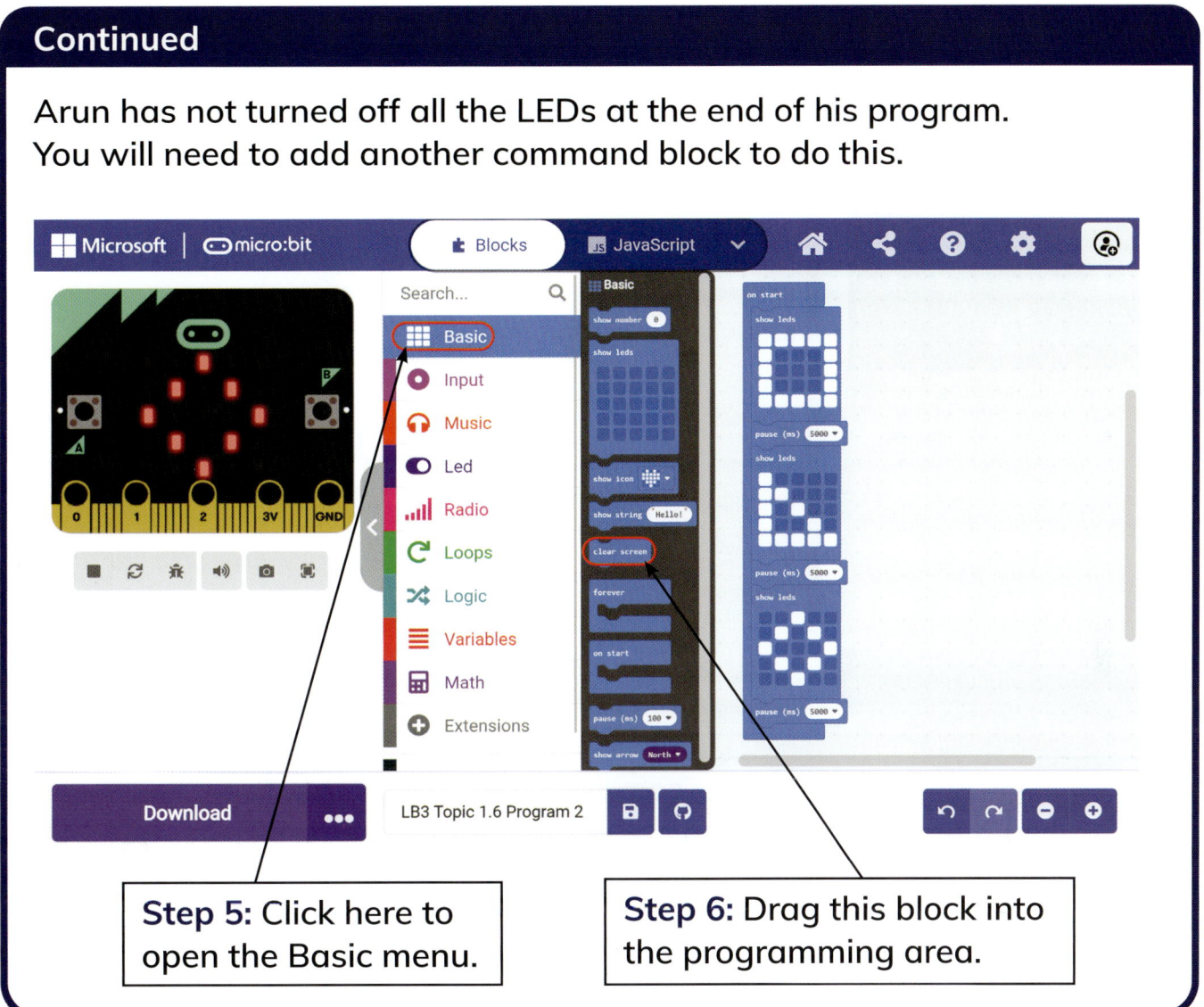

Step 5: Click here to open the Basic menu.

Step 6: Drag this block into the programming area.

1 Computational thinking and programming

Continued

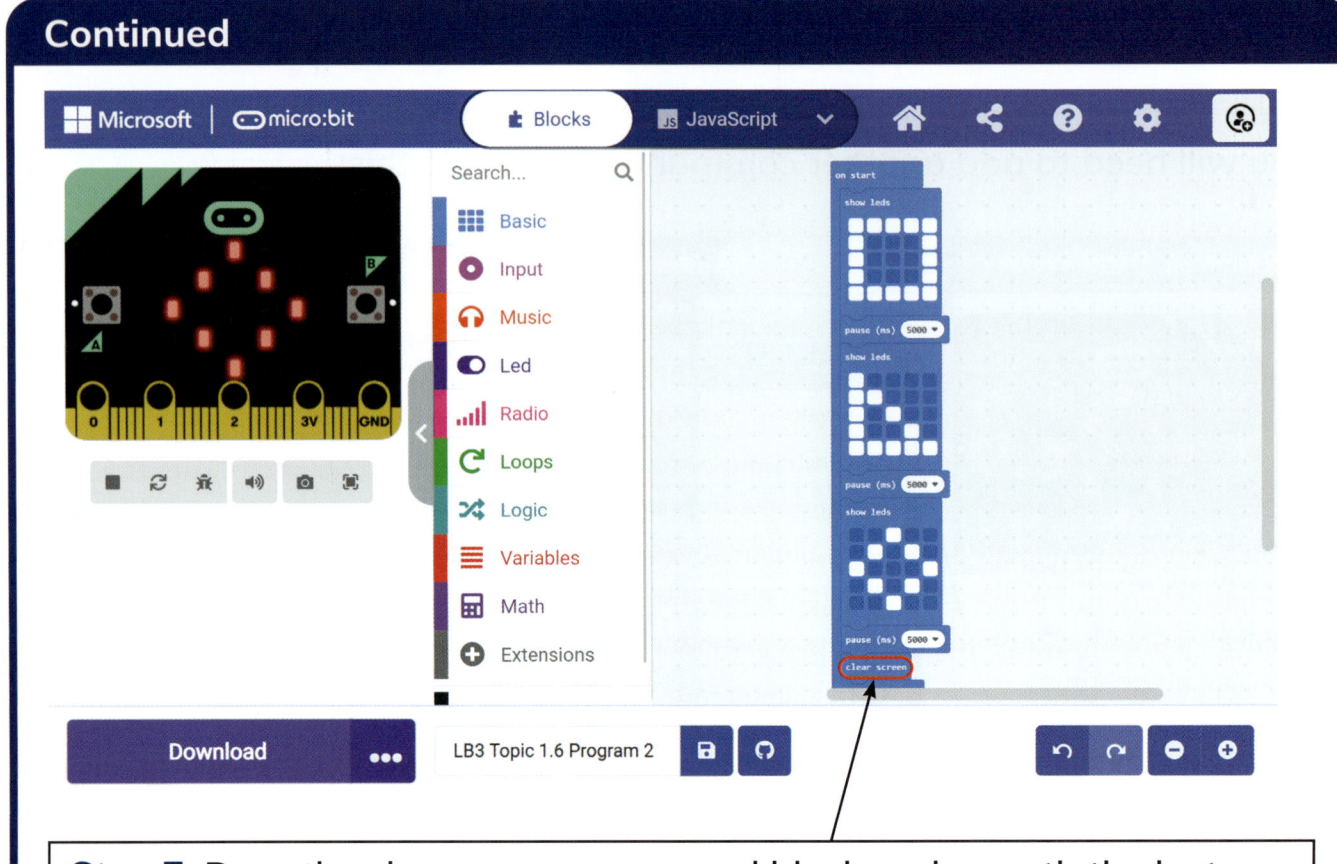

Step 7: Drag the clear screen command block underneath the last pause command block. When the grey shadow appears under the last pause command block, release the clear screen command block. Make sure the block is placed inside the 'on start' command block. This will turn all the LEDs off at the end of Arun's program.

1.6 Introducing the micro:bit

Activity 1

Input devices

> You will need:
> a desktop computer or laptop, a micro:bit, a micro USB B cable and access to the MakeCode website; or a tablet, a micro:bit, a battery pack and access to the MakeCode app, source file **1.15_input_devices** (needs to be already transferred onto the micro:bit), a pencil and paper or a whiteboard pen and mini whiteboard

You are going to find out how to use some of the micro:bit's input devices.

You need a micro:bit that already has the source file transferred to it.

The program has instructions that tell the micro:bit what to do when the buttons are pressed or when the micro:bit is shaken.

Remember that the output is what happens when the micro:bit follows the instructions.

Copy the table below.

Input	Output
Pressing button A	
Pressing button B	
Pressing buttons A and B together	
Shaking the micro:bit (accelerometer)	

93

Continued

Work with a partner to explore what happens when you use each of the inputs in the table.

Add the micro:bit's output for each input into your table.

You can write or draw what you see.

Remember that the micro:bit is following a certain program to tell it what to do for each input. So it will not always show these pictures when these inputs are used.

How am I doing?

Were you able to use the four different inputs?

Did you see a different picture when you used each input?

Input command blocks

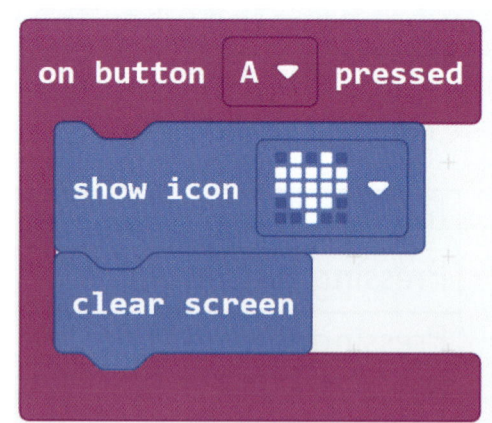

This is part of the program that was transferred to your micro:bit:

It starts with an input command block.

These can be found in the 'Input' category of the **toolbox**.

Now you are going to write a program that uses the micro:bit's input devices.

1.6 Introducing the micro:bit

Programming task 2

Using inputs in a program

> You will need:
> a desktop computer or laptop, a micro:bit, a micro USB B cable and access to the MakeCode website; or a tablet, a micro:bit, a battery pack and access to the MakeCode app, a pencil and paper or a whiteboard pen and mini whiteboard

First, choose two of the following inputs:

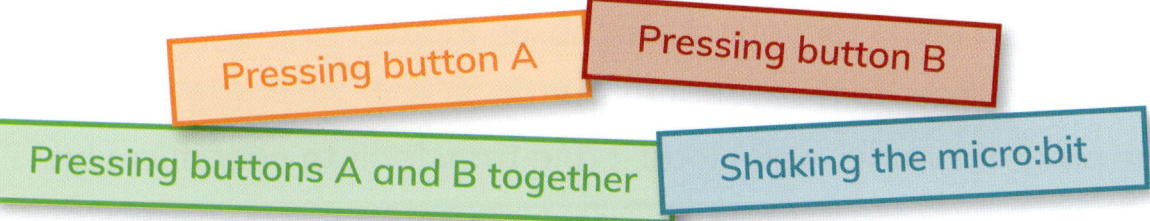

Next, choose an output to go with each input:

Now you are going to write a program that uses some of the micro:bit's input devices.

Step 1: Open MakeCode and click on 'New Project'.

Step 2: Give your project the name 'Using inputs'.

Step 3: Delete the 'on start' and 'forever' command blocks.

Step 4: Go the 'Input' category in the toolbox.

Find the command block for the input you have chosen.

My micro:bit will show a picture of a rabbit when it is shaken.

1   Computational thinking and programming

> **Continued**
>
> All of the 'button' inputs are in the command block called 'on button A pressed'.
>
> You can change which button or buttons are pressed using the arrow next to the 'A'.
>
> **Step 5:** Drag the command block you need into the programming area.
>
> **Step 6:** Add the 'show icon' command block from the 'Basic' category.
>
> Change it to show the icon that you have chosen for the input.
>
> Repeat these steps for your other chosen input.
>
> Use the simulator to test your program.
>
> If the program works, **download** it and transfer it to your micro:bit.

> **Stay safe!**
>
> When you transfer a program to the micro:bit, you download it from the internet.
>
> You should always check with an adult before downloading files from the internet.
>
> Some files can damage your computer.

Testing your programs

The micro:bit **simulator** is very useful because it allows you to test your program before downloading and transferring it to the micro:bit.

When we test a program, we check it to see if it does all the things we want it to do.

So we check to make sure we get the output we are expecting.

If we do not get the expected output, we can debug the program.

1.6 Introducing the micro:bit

Programming task 3

Debugging a program

> You will need:
> a desktop computer or laptop, a micro:bit, a micro USB B cable and access to the MakeCode website; or a tablet, a micro:bit, a battery pack and access to the MakeCode app, source file **1.16_debugging**, a pencil and paper or a whiteboard pen and mini whiteboard

Zara wants to write a program for her micro:bit. First, she has written down what she wants the micro:bit to do.

- Show a cross for two seconds when button B is pressed.
- Show a tick for two seconds when the micro:bit is shaken.

Here is the program Zara has written:

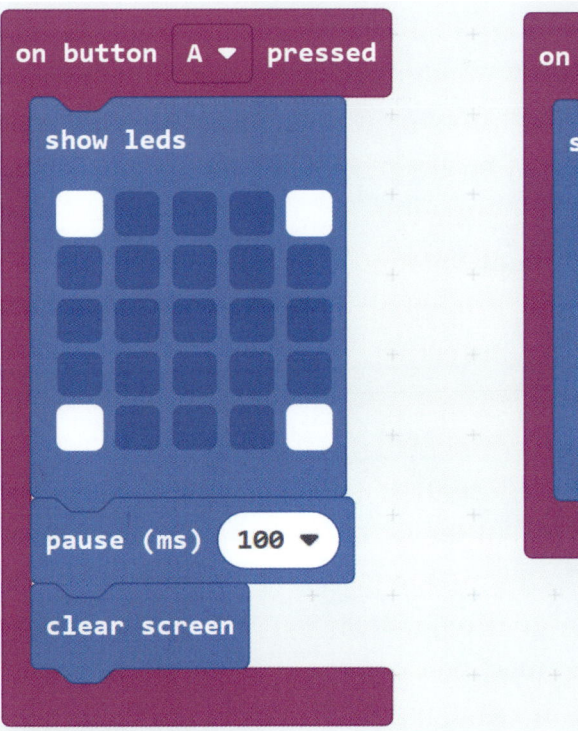

1 Computational thinking and programming

> **Continued**
>
> Work with a partner and look at Zara's program.
>
> 1 Which parts of her program has Zara done correctly?
>
> 2 Which parts of her program has Zara not done correctly?
>
> Now open the file your teacher gives you.
>
> Debug Zara's program so that it does everything she wrote down.

Look what I can do!

- ☐ I can program a micro:bit to show pictures using its LEDs.
- ☐ I can write programs that control the micro:bit's lights.
- ☐ I can download and transfer a program to a micro:bit.
- ☐ I can write programs that use the micro:bit's input devices.
- ☐ I know why testing programs is important.
- ☐ I can test and debug programs.

1.6 Introducing the micro:bit

Project

Showing feelings on the micro:bit

> You will need:
> a desktop computer or laptop, a micro:bit, a micro USB B cable and access to the MakeCode website; or a tablet, a micro:bit, a battery pack and access to the MakeCode app, printout of source file **1.13_microbit_grid**, colouring pen or pencil, a pencil and paper or a whiteboard pen and mini whiteboard

Have you ever been in a lesson where you did not understand something?

Have you felt worried about telling your teacher that you did not understand in front of your classmates?

If the answer is yes, do not worry. Lots of children feel the same way.

However, it is really useful for your teacher to know how confident you feel with the learning that you are doing.

A micro:bit could help you share this information with your teacher without having to put your hand up.

Using three different inputs, the micro:bit could show a picture to let your teacher know if you are feeling:

- confident
- a little unsure
- worried that you do not understand.

You are going to work with a partner to complete this project.

Working with other people when you are writing programs is useful.

> **Continued**
>
> Can you remember why?
>
> The project has been split up into smaller parts to help you complete it.
>
> Complete each of the steps below.
>
> **Step 1:** Think of the three pictures that you are going to show on the micro:bit screen.
>
> You can use source file **1.13_microbit_grid** to draw them.
>
> **Step 2:** Write an algorithm to say which input you will use to show each picture.
>
> **Step 3:** Write the program using MakeCode.
>
> Remember to swap the roles of writing the code and checking the code with your partner.
>
> **Step 4:** Use the simulator to test the program and debug it if necessary.
>
> **Step 5:** Download the file and transfer it to your micro:bit.

1.6 Introducing the micro:bit

Check your progress

1 Zara is at the park. There is a map of the park below.

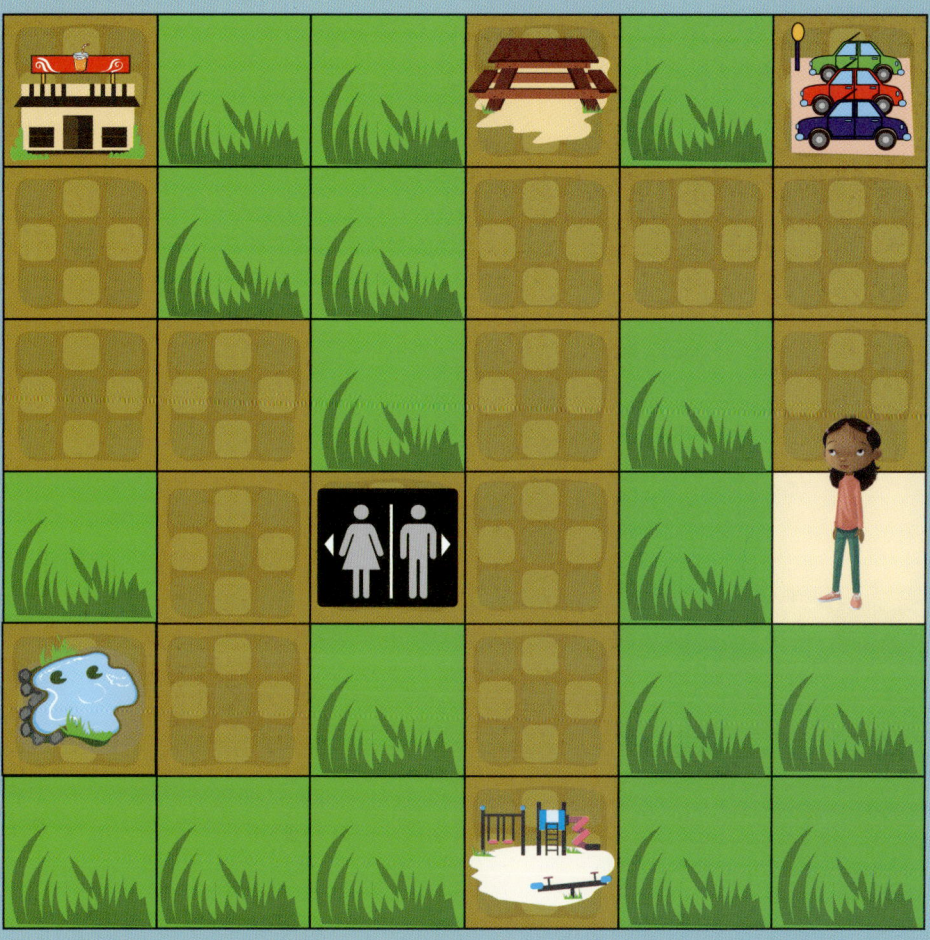

She has tried using the algorithm below to get to the playground, but it did not work.

Correct the algorithm so that Zara gets to the playground.

1 Face north.
2 Go forward 2 squares.
3 Face east.
4 Go forward 2 squares.
5 Face south.
6 Go forward 3 squares.

101

1 Computational thinking and programming

Continued

2 Marcus has written this program in Scratch:

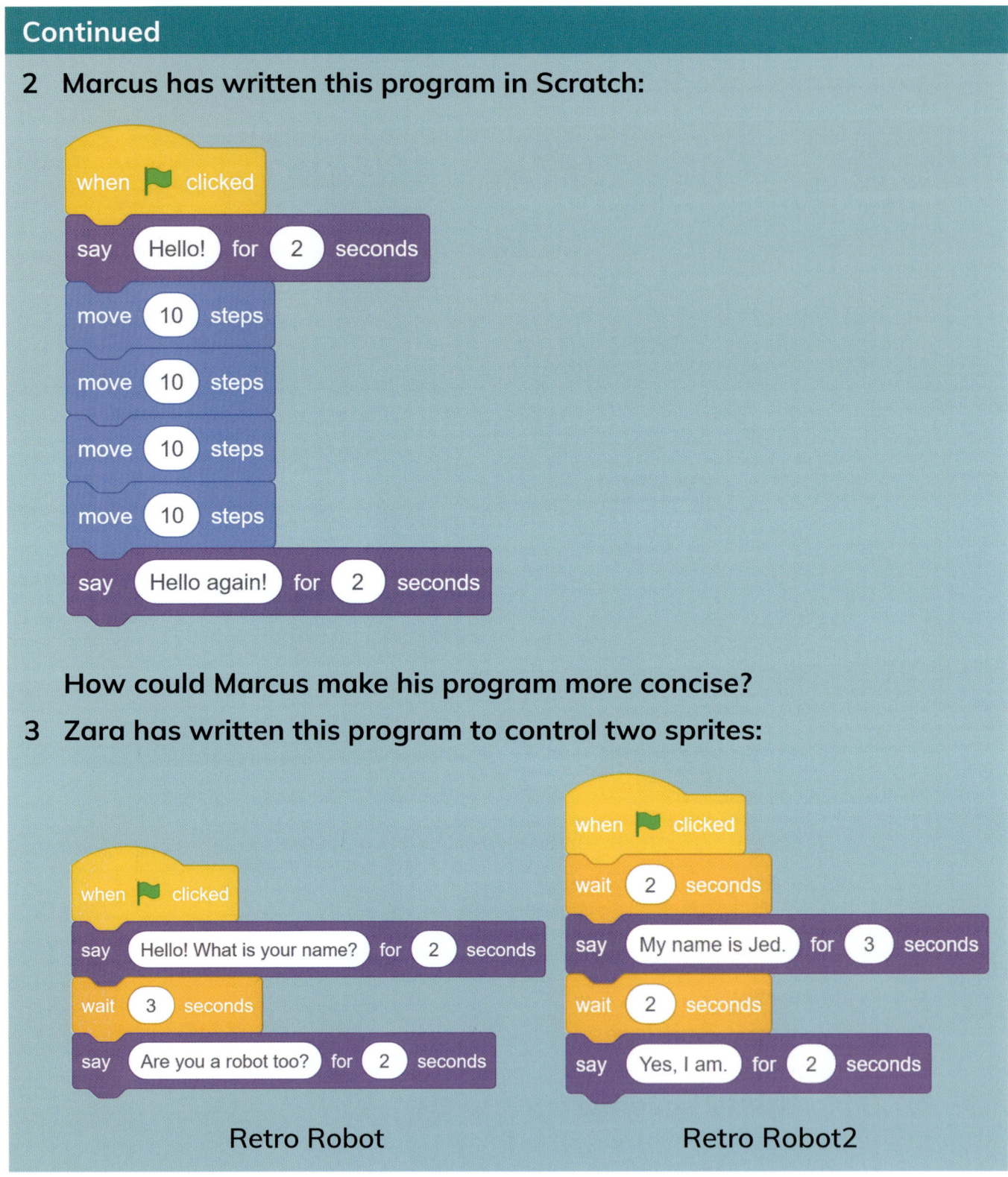

How could Marcus make his program more concise?

3 Zara has written this program to control two sprites:

Continued

Copy and complete the following sentences, adding the name of the correct sprite: Retro Robot or Retro Robot2.

a _____ will start speaking first.

b _____ will wait 2 seconds before speaking.

c _____ will be the last sprite to speak.

4 Here is a program for the micro:bit.

The program has two parts. Each part of the program uses an input.

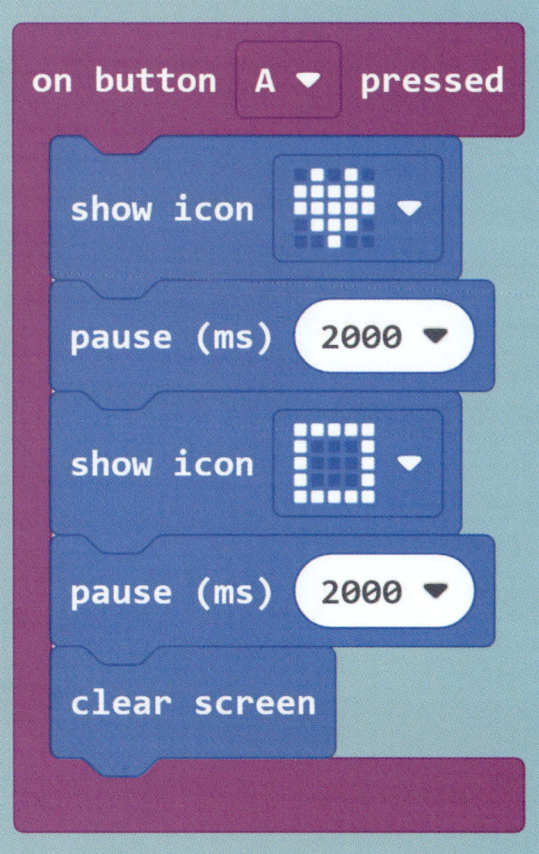

Part 1

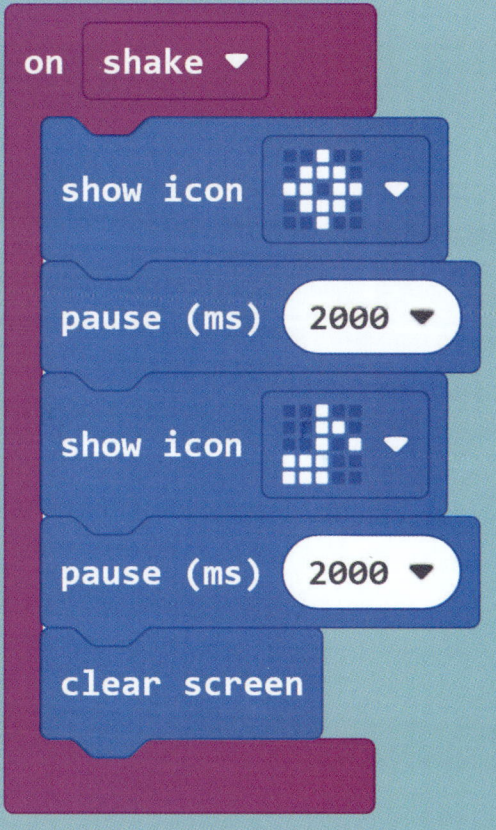

Part 2

1 Computational thinking and programming

> **Continued**
>
> Look at the statements below. Decide if each one is true for Part 1, Part 2 or both parts.
>
> a A picture is shown on the micro:bit's LEDs.
>
> b When a button is pressed, an image is shown on the micro:bit.
>
> c When the micro:bit is shaken, an image is shown on the micro:bit.
>
> d The LEDs are turned off at the end of the program.

2 > Managing data

> 2.1 How data can help us

We are going to:
- look at how we can find answers to problems by collecting and understanding data
- choose the correct data to help find the answers to problems.

> collect   interpret
> data   select

Getting started

What do you already know?
- You understand the difference between statistical and non-statistical questions.
- You can answer questions using different types of data (facts).
- You have used data to solve problems.

Now try this!

Imagine your school has been given some money to spend on sports equipment like footballs, tennis racquets and hockey sticks.

The headteacher is going to let the children decide what to spend the money on.

How could you find out what everyone wants to spend the money on?

Discuss with a partner.

105

2 Managing data

How can data help?

Arun is going to decorate and sell notebooks to people in his school to raise money for charity.

Arun can only sell two different coloured notebooks in his shop.

The problem is, there are lots of different colours to choose from!

Arun has decided to **collect** data to help him decide which colours to sell.

Arun collected data from 30 learners about their favourite colour.

He will show his data using a block graph.

Collect means to get things and bring them together. Remember that a piece of data is a fact. It can be a word, number or picture.

2.1 How data can help us

You have already learnt about block graphs.

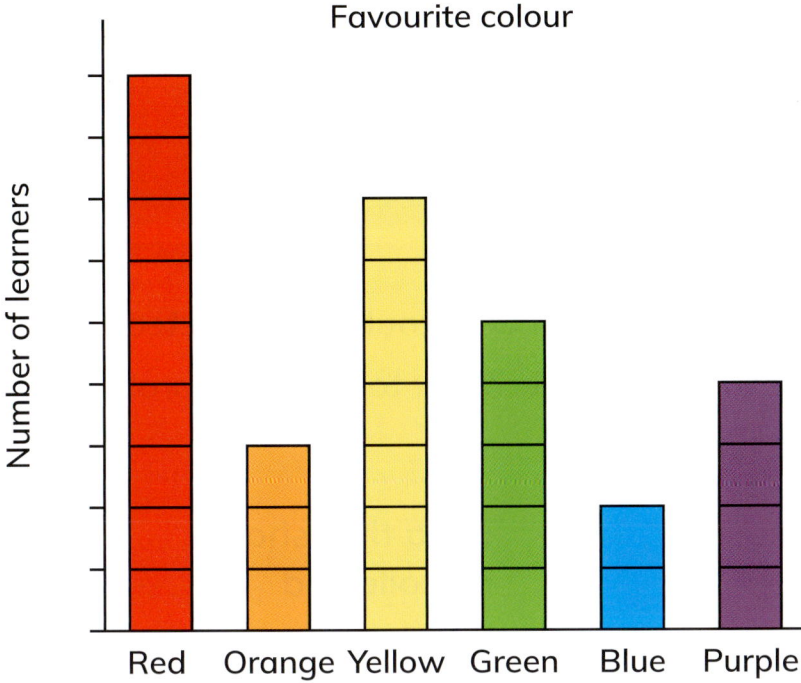

Now Arun can **interpret** his data.

When we interpret something, we try to understand what it means or what it is telling us.

Arun sees from his graph that red and yellow are the most popular colours.

This is an example of where collecting and interpreting data can help us with a problem.

The data in the graph suggests that if I choose red and yellow, I will sell the most notebooks.

2 Managing data

Unplugged activity 1

Which data could help?

> **You will need:**
> a pencil and paper or a whiteboard pen and mini whiteboard

Look at the information below.

There are five problems and five sets of data that could be collected.

Match each problem with the data you would collect to solve the problem.

Write down the letter that matches each number.

Problem

1. Marcus wants to make an animation in ScratchJr for young children, but he does not know which character to use.

2. The headteacher needs to think of a new school logo, but he does not know which colour most of the learners would like.

3. Zara wants to write a story that lots of children will enjoy, but she does not know what type of story to write.

4. Sofia wants to make a decorated photo frame, but she doesn't know how big to make it.

5. Arun wants to think up a dance for young children, but he doesn't know which music to choose.

Data that should be collected

A Children's favourite type of story

B The most common size of photo

C Young children's favourite character in ScratchJr

D Young children's favourite music

E Learners' favourite colours

2.1 How data can help us

> **Continued**
>
> **How am I doing?**
>
> Compare your list with a partner.
>
> Draw a smiley face for each answer that is the same as your partner's answer.
>
> Discuss any answers that are different.

When is data not helpful?

Collecting and interpreting data cannot help to solve all problems.

Arun has chosen the two colours for the notebooks he will sell.

He also wants to decorate his notebooks.

Collecting data could help with this in some ways:

- Arun can collect data to find out what learners' favourite decorations are.
- He can decorate some notebooks and collect data to find out which designs learners like best.

However, Arun will need to use his imagination when he is decorating the notebooks.

He will have lots of creative ideas!

He does not need to collect data for this part of the task.

109

2 Managing data

Unplugged activity 2

When data cannot help

> You will need:
> a pencil and paper or a whiteboard pen and mini whiteboard

Below are three problems from the same list from Unplugged activity 1.

You know you could collect data to solve part of each problem.

But data cannot help with other parts of the problems.

Discuss with a partner which part of each problem cannot be solved using data, and why.

Problems

1. Marcus wants to make an animation in ScratchJr for young children. He cannot use data to…

   a find children's favourite Scratch character

   b write the story

   c find out how many children use Scratch

2. Sofia wants to make a decorated photo frame. She cannot use data to…

   a help her decide which pattern to decorate it with

   b find the most common size of photo frame

   c find out how many people need a new photo frame

2.1 How data can help us

> **Continued**
>
> 3 Arun wants to think up a dance for young children.
>   He cannot use data to...
>
>   a find out the most popular music for young children
>
>   b make up some new dance moves
>
>   c find out how many children go to a dance class
>
> Did you notice that data is less helpful for creative tasks, like decorating things and using your imagination?
>
> **How am I doing?**
>
> Swap your answers with another pair of learners.
>
> Draw a smiley face if you agree with what they have written.
>
> Discuss any answers that you disagree with. Explain why you disagree.

Data about you

We can collect data about many different things.

Think about how much data someone could collect about you.

They could collect information about your:

- hair colour
- eye colour
- height
- favourite food
- favourite colour
- favourite hobby.

Tell a partner three more things someone could find out about you.

111

2 Managing data

Questions

1. Write down two problems that can be solved by collecting data.
2. Write down one problem that cannot be solved by collecting data.

> **Did you know?**
>
> Data about you is collected when you are using the internet.
>
> If you search for something online, like a pair of trainers, you might then start to see adverts for trainers when you are online.
>
> Shops have paid for the adverts.
>
> They hope that you will click on the advert and buy the trainers from them.

Choosing the right data

When lots of data is available, it is important to **select** (choose) the right data to help us solve a problem.

Marcus has collected lots of data about the learners in his class.

He has collected this data about his classmates:

- favourite film

- favourite school subject

- favourite animal

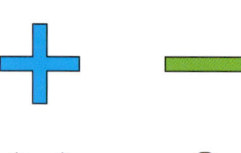

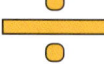

2.1 How data can help us

- sports they like

- eye colour

- hair colour

- height

- how many pets they have

- their hobbies

- where they live.

Marcus wants to set up a sports club on a field near his house.

Marcus can only have 10 children at his club.

He plans to use the data he has collected to choose which children to invite.

Some of the data Marcus has collected will be more useful than the rest.

Sofia has suggested which data she thinks would help Marcus to choose which children to invite.

Do you agree with her?

1 sports they like

2 their hobbies

3 where they live

4 hair colour

2 Managing data

Marcus agrees with Sofia's first three ideas, because:

- he can see which sports learners would like to play in the club
- he will know which learners might want to join if they have sport as a hobby
- he can see which learners live near him so it will be easy to meet at the field.

However, Marcus doesn't agree with Sofia's last suggestion, because it doesn't matter what hair colour they have!

This data is not important for Marcus's problem.

Stay safe!

The data Marcus has collected is personal data.

Marcus should keep this data safe and not share it with anyone.

When you are online, always ask an adult before sharing personal data.

Unplugged activity 3

Which data will solve it?

> You will need:
> a pencil and paper or a whiteboard pen and mini whiteboard

Part 1

Your teacher will put you in teams of four and take you to the hall or an open space.

Your teacher will write the 10 sets of data Marcus has collected on individual bits of paper and stick them up around the hall.

Your teacher will now read each of the problems below, one at a time.

When your teacher reads the problem, quickly discuss in your team which data would help solve the problem and run to stand by it.

2.1 How data can help us

Continued

Different team members can run to different sets of data when more than one will help.

Discuss with your teacher why you think the data you have chosen will help to solve that problem.

Are there any differences between groups you can discuss?

Problems

1. Zara's teacher wants to pair up learners who have the same hobbies and live near each other, but she doesn't know what everyone likes and where they live.

2. The headteacher wants to know who is in the class photo, but she cannot remember what all the learners look like.

3. The sports teacher wants to group learners who enjoy the same sports together.

4. Sofia's teacher wants to encourage learners to help each other with their homework. She wants to pair learners with the same favourite subject who live near each other.

2 Managing data

> **Continued**
>
> Part 2
>
> Look at the three sets of data that were not used in Part 1.
>
> In your teams, write a problem that could be solved by collecting these sets of data.
>
> Share your ideas with the rest of the class.

You have learnt about selecting the right data and ignoring data that is not useful for solving a problem.

This is an important skill when you are learning as you are often given lots of information and need to find the most important points.

Can you think of any times when you have had to do this, such as researching key facts about a topic online?

Look what I can do!

☐ I know how we can find answers to problems by collecting and understanding data.

☐ I can choose the correct data to help find the answers to problems.

> 2.2 Super spreadsheets

We are going to:
- learn that spreadsheets are made from rows and columns
- understand that data can be entered into cells in spreadsheets
- record and represent data in spreadsheets
- understand how to format cells in spreadsheets.

Getting started

What do you already know?
- Data can be stored on computers.
- You have used forms to gather data.
- You have entered data into a table.
- You have made a block graph to present data.

bar chart   icon
cell   present
column   row
data   spreadsheet
format

2 Managing data

Continued

Now try this!

Look at the block graph below.

It is like the graphs you have made before.

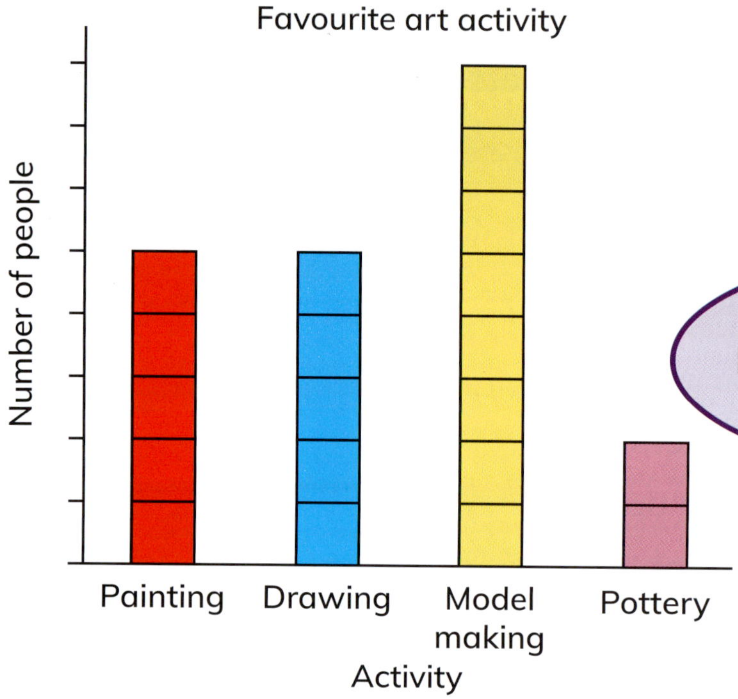

Favourite art activity

(Block graph showing Number of people vs Activity: Painting = 4, Drawing = 4, Model making = 8, Pottery = 2)

Remember, with a block graph, each block represents 1.

Discuss with a partner:
1. What data has been collected?
2. Which is the most popular activity?
3. Which is the least popular activity?
4. How many people have been asked in total?

2.2 Super spreadsheets

Introducing spreadsheets

A **spreadsheet** is a type of computer program.

You can add data to spreadsheets.

Spreadsheets have lots of **cells** in them.

Cells are boxes where data can be entered.

A **column** is a group of cells that go down.

They look like columns in a building:

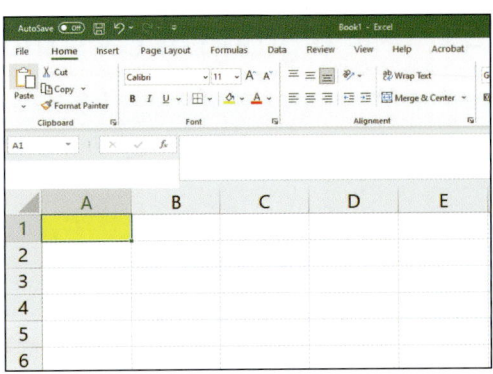

column

The top of each column in a spreadsheet has a letter, starting with A.

Question

1 What is the letter of the column shown here?

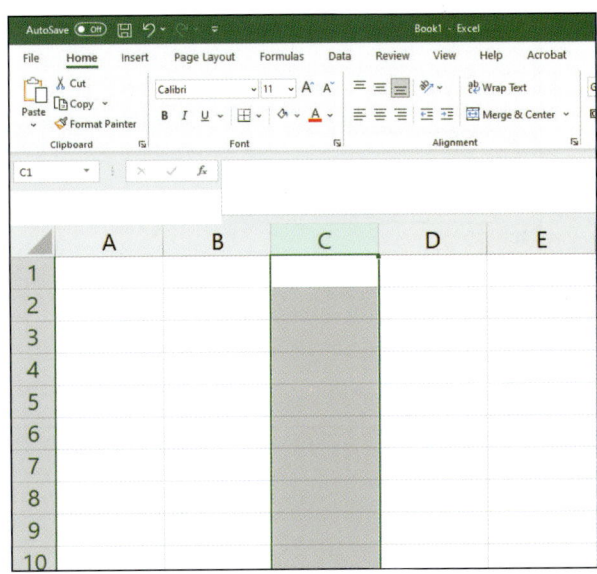

119

2 Managing data

A **row** is a group of cells that go across.

 ← row

The left-hand side of each row in a spreadsheet is labelled with a number, starting at 1.

Question

2 What is the number of the row that is highlighted below?

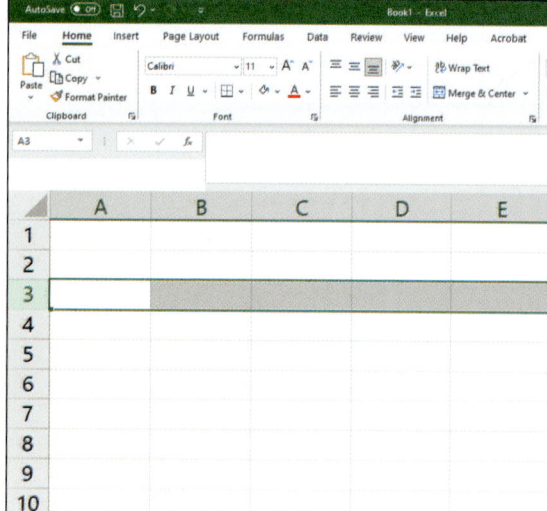

2.2 Super spreadsheets

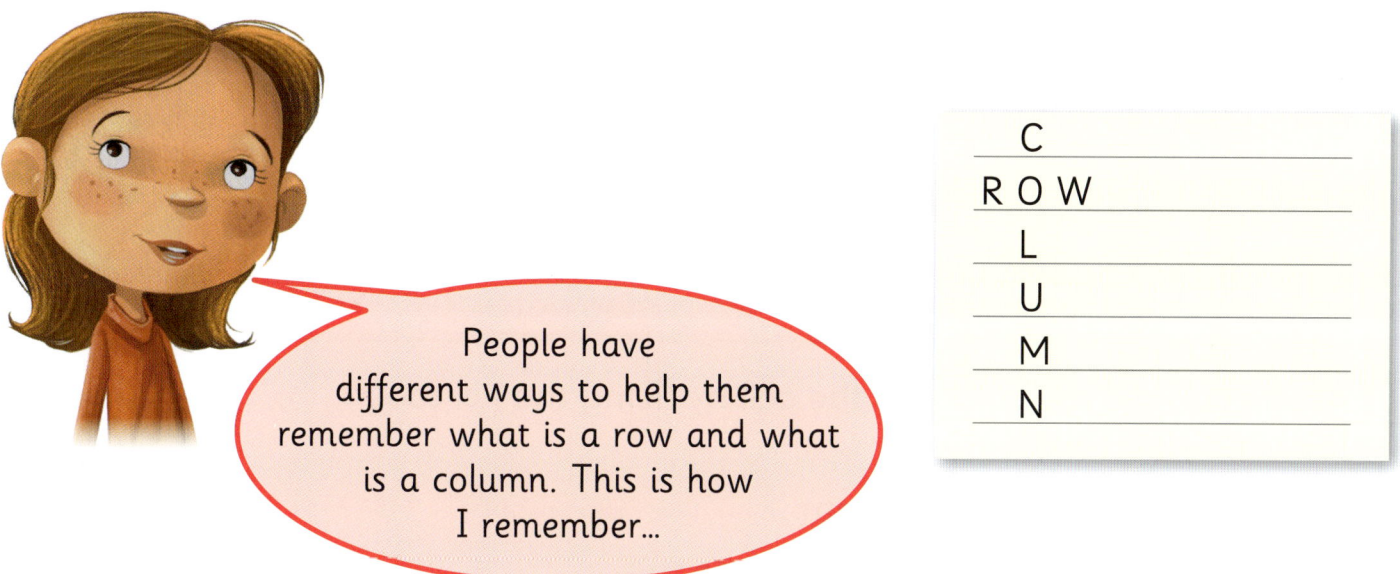

People have different ways to help them remember what is a row and what is a column. This is how I remember…

We can use the letter at the top of the column and the number at the start of the row to name each cell.

A cell in the picture below has been filled red.

The cell is in column C and on row 3, so the name of the cell is C3.

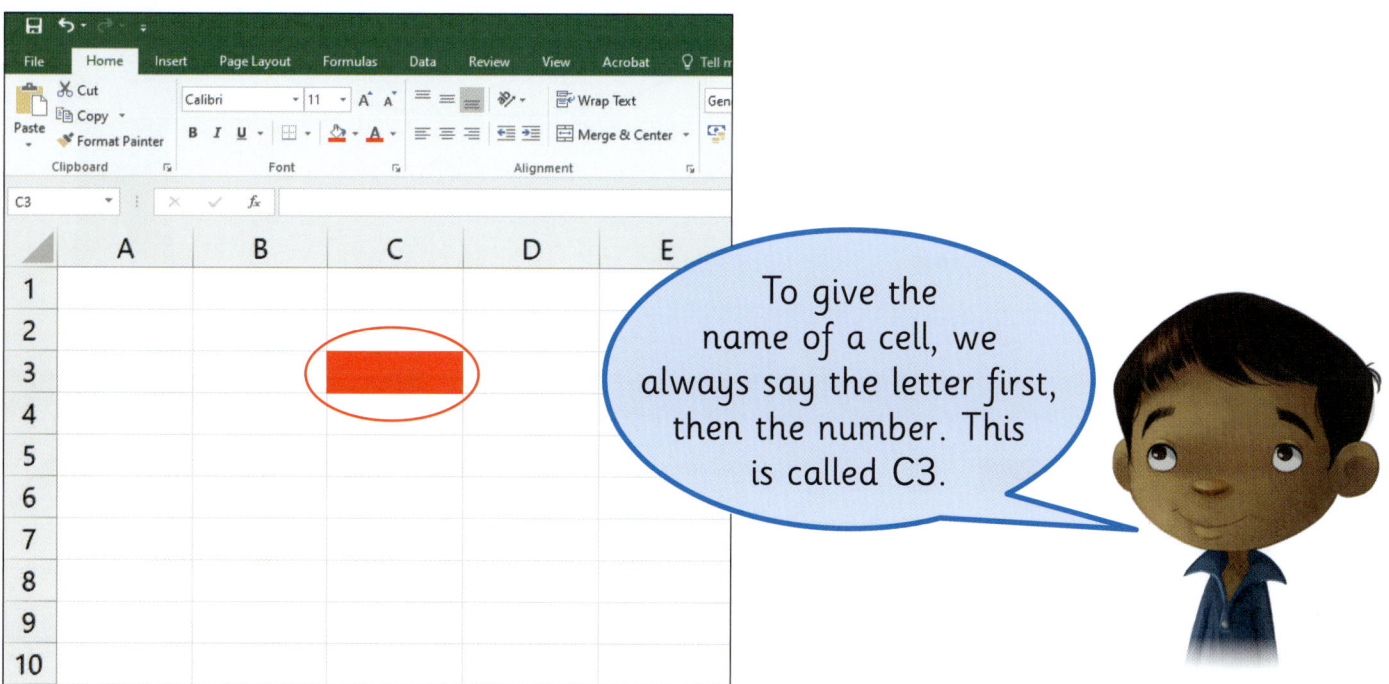

To give the name of a cell, we always say the letter first, then the number. This is called C3.

2 Managing data

Activity 1

Spreadsheet sketches

> **You will need:**
> a desktop computer, laptop or tablet, a spreadsheet program (for example, Microsoft Excel), timer or stopwatch

Arun changed the colour of the cell by using the Fill tool. Now it's your turn!

Open the spreadsheet program.

Your teacher will show you how to do this.

Step 1: Choose the cell you wish to fill by clicking on it. Start with cell C3.

Click on the small downward arrow beside the **icon** of a bucket pouring paint.

Step 2: Next, choose a colour.

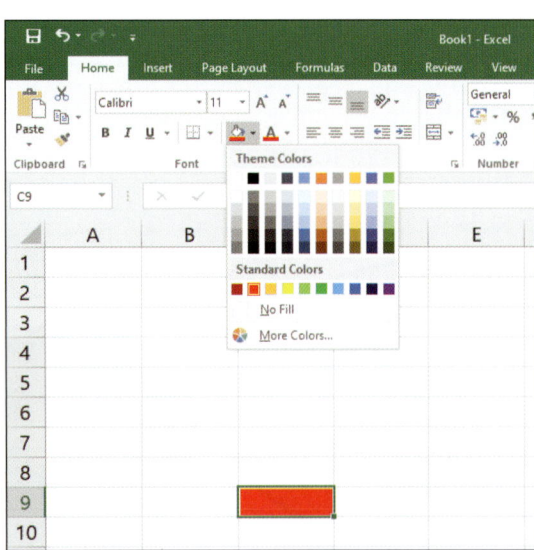

Remember, an icon is a small picture of something.

Now you are going to draw a picture in the spreadsheet.

2.2 Super spreadsheets

Continued

Step 3: After you have filled cell C3, change the colour of these cells:

C10, B9, D5, D6, D7, D11, E3, E10, F9

What is the picture of?

Step 4: Now clear your spreadsheet by choosing all of the cells you have filled.

To do this, click on cell B3, then hold down the mouse button and drag the pointer down to cell F11, so your whole picture is chosen.

Click the arrow beside the icon of the Fill tool again and choose 'No Fill'.

Draw your own simple picture by filling some of the cells.

You could draw a car, an aeroplane or a boat.

Try not to use more than 15 cells.

Write down the names of the coloured cells you have used to draw your picture.

Clear your spreadsheet.

Swap your list of cell names with a partner.

Use their instructions to draw their picture in your spreadsheet.

How am I doing?

Work with a partner.

Take turns to point at a cell on a spreadsheet.

See how quickly the other person can say the name of the cell.

2 Managing data

Continued

Draw a tick for each one you get right.

See how many correct answers you can get as a pair in 30 seconds.

Compare how many you got with another pair. Who got more?

Can you do it again and get even more in 30 seconds?

Did you know?

The maximum number of rows in Microsoft's Excel spreadsheet program is currently 1,048,576.

It would take about a whole day to scroll down to the bottom if you just used the down arrow!

Adding data to a spreadsheet

Data can be entered (added) into cells in a spreadsheet.

Sofia has collected data from her friends about their favourite hobby.

She has recorded this in a table.

Favourite hobby	Number of children
Playing sport	6
Reading	6
Collecting things	8
Playing video games	10

2.2 Super spreadsheets

Sofia is going to enter this data into a spreadsheet.

First, Sofia enters the table headings in cells A1 and B1.

She does this by clicking on each cell in turn and typing the headings.

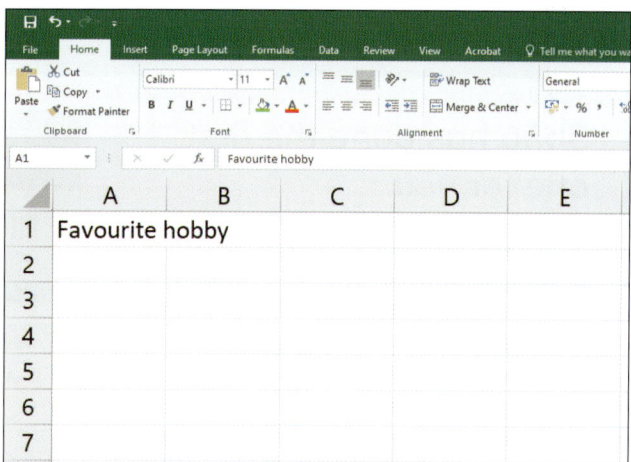

You can make a column wider to fit more letters in.

Use the mouse to put the pointer on the right-hand edge of the column.

This needs to be in the top row, where the column letters are.

The pointer will change to a cross with two arrows, like this: ✛

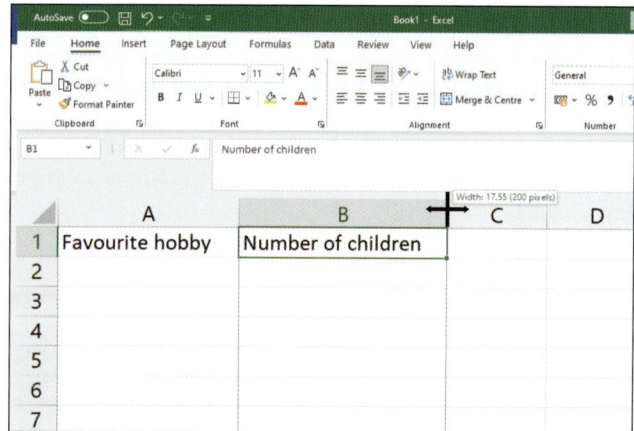

Now you can click and drag the column to make it wider.

Sofia needs your help to enter the rest of the data.

Practical task 1

Entering Sofia's data into a spreadsheet

> You will need:
> a desktop computer, laptop or tablet, a spreadsheet program (for example, Microsoft Excel), source file **2.1_hobbies**

Open the file your teacher gives you.

It has the table headings that Sofia has already entered.

Enter the different hobbies and the number of children choosing each hobby as their favourite.

125

2 Managing data

> **Continued**
>
> Sofia has done the first one for you.
>
> Make sure you save your completed spreadsheet.
>
> To do this, click on the 'Save' icon.
>
> You can give it a different title or keep the same title.
>
>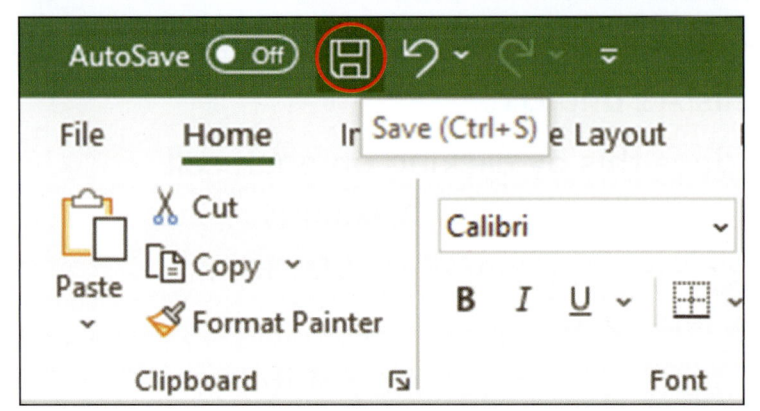
>
> Your teacher will tell you where to save your spreadsheet.
>
> **How am I doing?**
>
> Work with a partner.
>
> Draw a smiley face if your table looks the same as your partner's table.
>
> Discuss any differences.

Formatting cells

In this topic, you have entered words and numbers into cells.

The **format** is the way the information is shown.

We can see this with dates. Dates are often shown as 14/09/2023, 14 September 2023 or 14.9.23.

Changing the format of data in cells can make spreadsheets easier to read.

It also tells the spreadsheet what type of data is in each cell.

Zara has a spreadsheet recording the money her school has raised for charities at three events during the year.

2.2 Super spreadsheets

Her spreadsheet is shown below.

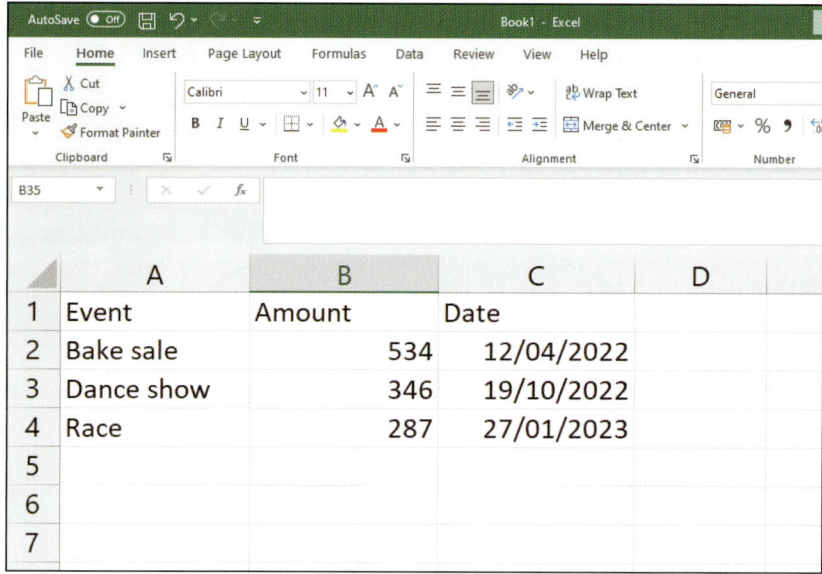

Look at the 'Amount' column.

It is not very easy to understand what the numbers in this column mean.

They might mean the amount of people at each event.

The numbers in these cells actually show the amount of money each event raised in dollars.

We need to format the numbers as dollars with a dollar sign in front to make this clear.

2 Managing data

First, Zara selects the cells she wants to format.

Zara clicks on the first cell, then holds down the mouse button and drags the pointer across the other cells she wants to format.

A box appears around the cells to show what is selected.

Then Zara chooses the 'Home' tab at the top of the screen, finds the 'Number' section and clicks on the arrow next to the word 'General'.

> If you only want to format one cell, you just need to click on it.

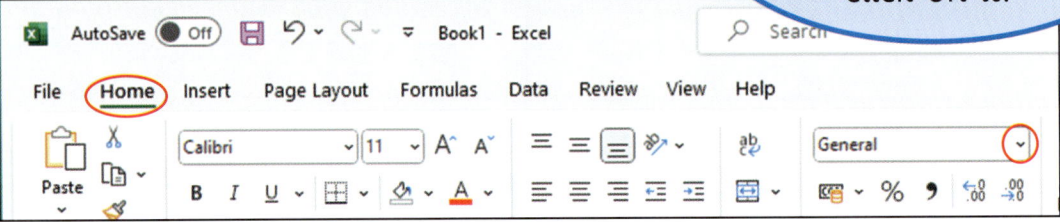

This opens a menu. Zara clicks on 'Currency' – this is another word for money.

This will allow her to change the currency to the currency of her home country.

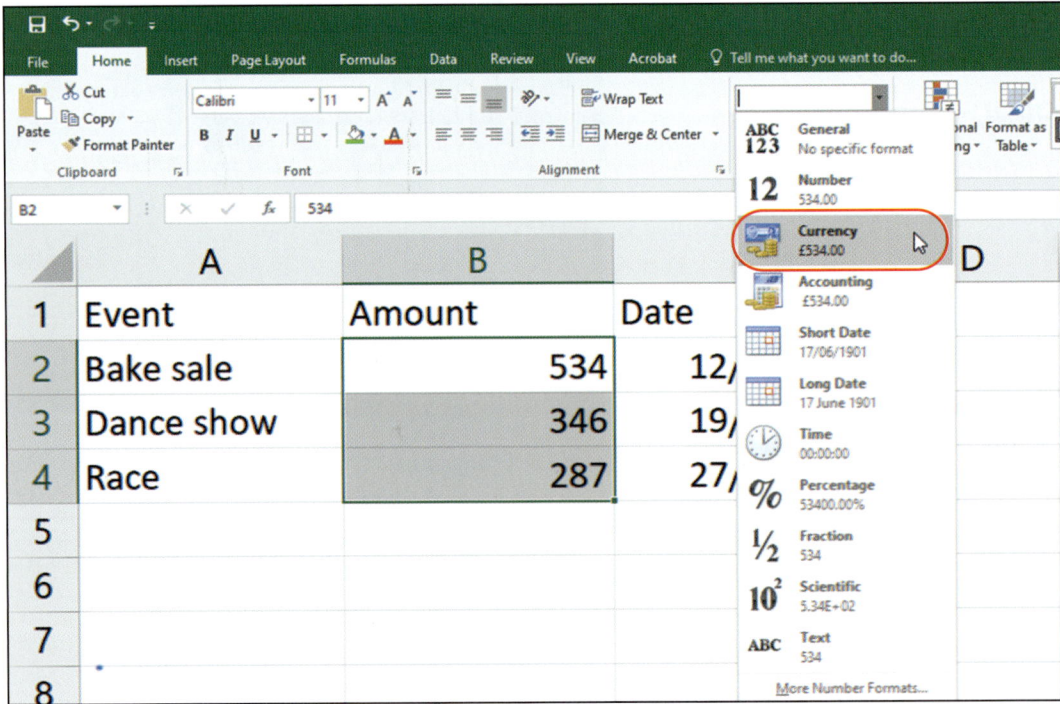

128

2.2 Super spreadsheets

The cells in this column are now formatted as dollars.

Zara's teacher has asked her to format the cells in the 'Date' column to show the month as a word.

It is currently formatted as a number.

Zara repeats the steps above, but this time she selects the cells in the 'Date' column.

When she clicks on the arrow next to 'General', Zara chooses 'Long Date' instead of 'Currency'.

If Zara wanted to go back to showing the date as 12/04/2022, she could choose 'Short Date'.

We can also format the words in cells.

This can be useful to make table headings stand out.

To do this, Zara uses the 'Font' section at the top of the screen, which is also part of the 'Home' tab. Font means the typed letters.

B
Amount
$534.00
$346.00
$287.00

	A	B	C
1	Event	Amount	Date
2	Bake sale	$534.00	12 April 2022
3	Dance show	$346.00	19 October 2022
4	Race	$287.00	27 January 2023

2 Managing data

This menu changes the font.

These buttons change the font size: a larger number makes it bigger, a smaller number makes it smaller.

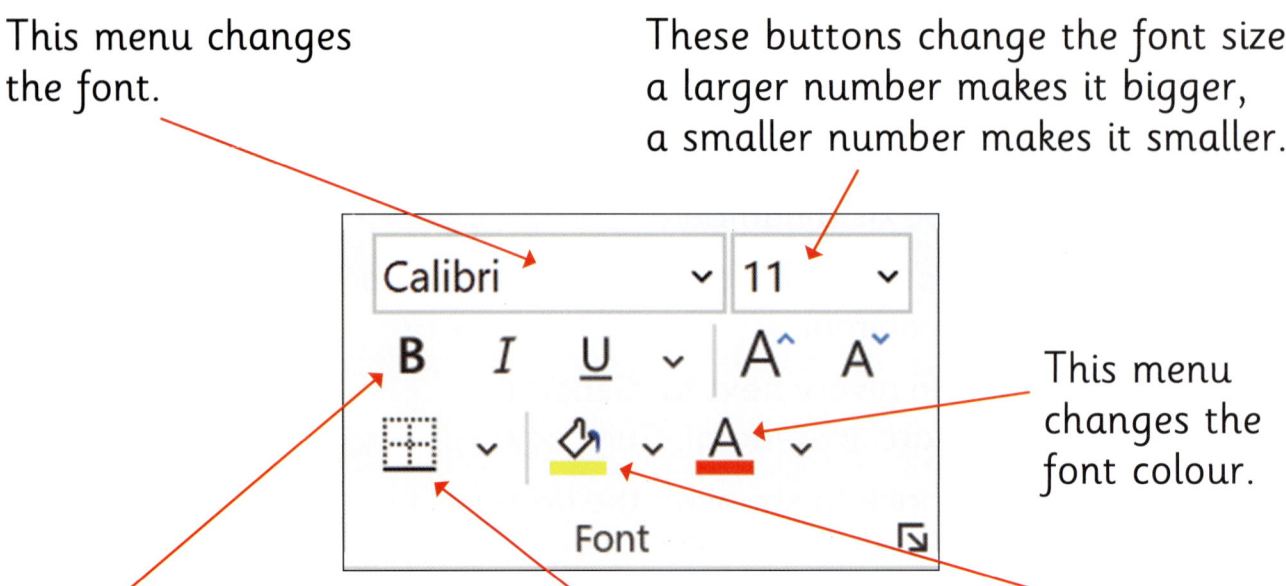

This menu changes the font colour.

These buttons change the style of the font:
B makes it **bold**,
I makes it *italic* and
U underlines it.

This menu adds lines (borders) to the cells.

This menu changes the cell colour – we used it earlier in the topic.

Zara has made three format changes to the spreadsheet headings.

Can you see them?

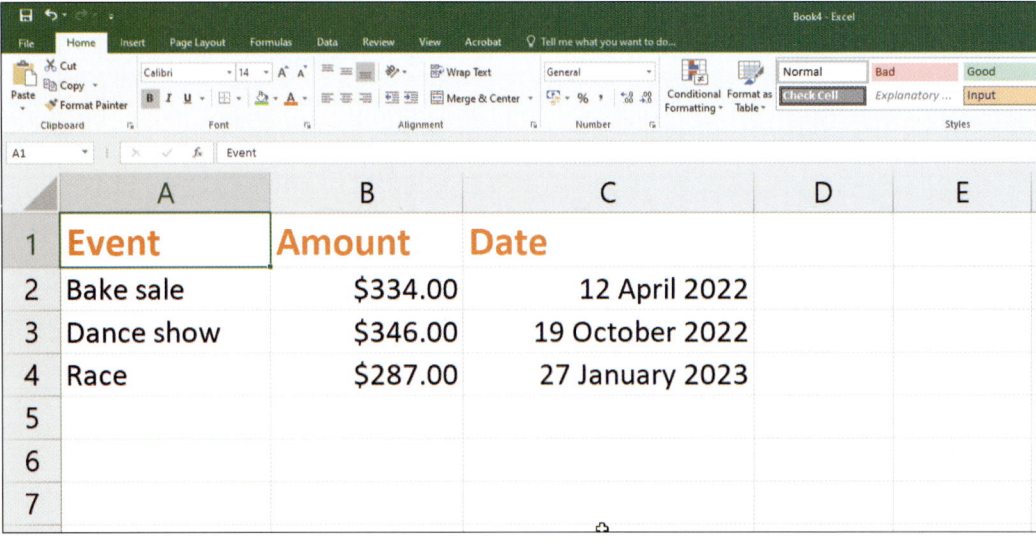

130

2.2 Super spreadsheets

Zara has:
- made the heading font bigger
- changed the colour from black to orange
- made the font bold.

She did this by selecting the cells and using the buttons in the 'Font' section.

Question

3   Look back at the picture of the 'Font' section. Can you point to the buttons Sofia used to change the formatting?

> **Practical task 2**
>
> **Format a spreadsheet**
>
> You will need:
> a desktop computer, laptop or tablet, a spreadsheet program (for example, Microsoft Excel), source file **2.2_pocket_money**
>
> Marcus has made a spreadsheet to show everything he has spent his pocket money on this month.
>
> He shows it to Arun, but Arun does not think it is very easy to understand.
>
> *I think Marcus should format his spreadsheet to help me to understand it.*
>
> Open the file your teacher gives you.
>
> Help Marcus by formatting these things:
> - Format the currency of the prices so they are shown in the currency of your country.
> - Format the dates so they show the month as a word.
> - Format the headings so they are bold, a bigger font size, and a different colour.

2 Managing data

> **Continued**
>
> **How am I doing?**
>
> Could you remember how to format everything?
>
> Give yourself a tick for each thing that you correctly formatted.

Presenting data

We can use spreadsheet software to **present** (show) data.

The way we present data can help us to understand it.

When we see data as a chart or graph, we can often understand it more quickly and easily than looking at a table.

A **bar chart** is similar to a block graph, which you have made before.

In a block graph, each column of data has lines to show the blocks.

A bar chart does not have separate blocks. We use bars (rectangles) instead.

In both bar charts and block graphs, we can compare data by looking at the heights of the bars.

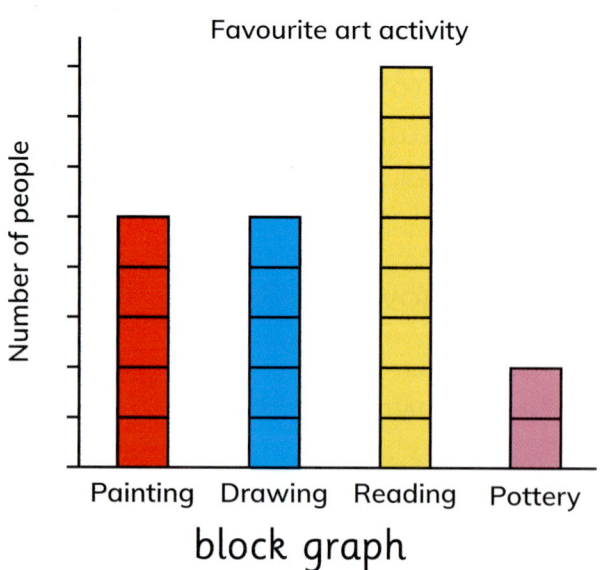

block graph

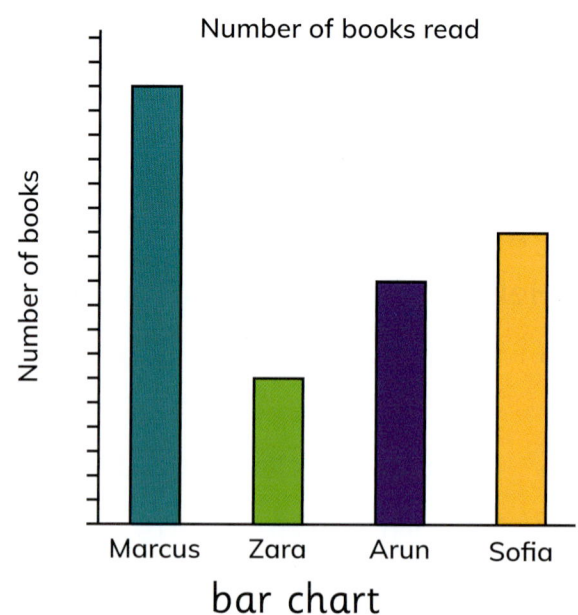

bar chart

2.2 Super spreadsheets

Spreadsheets can create bar charts for us.

Zara has collected data on the number of books she and her friends have read in six months.

She has added this data to a spreadsheet.

Zara uses the spreadsheet to present the data as a bar chart.

In the graphs and charts you have already looked at, the numbers on the left go up by one each time.

But when we have larger numbers in our data, there may not be space for this.

The numbers may go up by two, five or ten at a time.

Look carefully, as each step on a bar chart may be more than one.

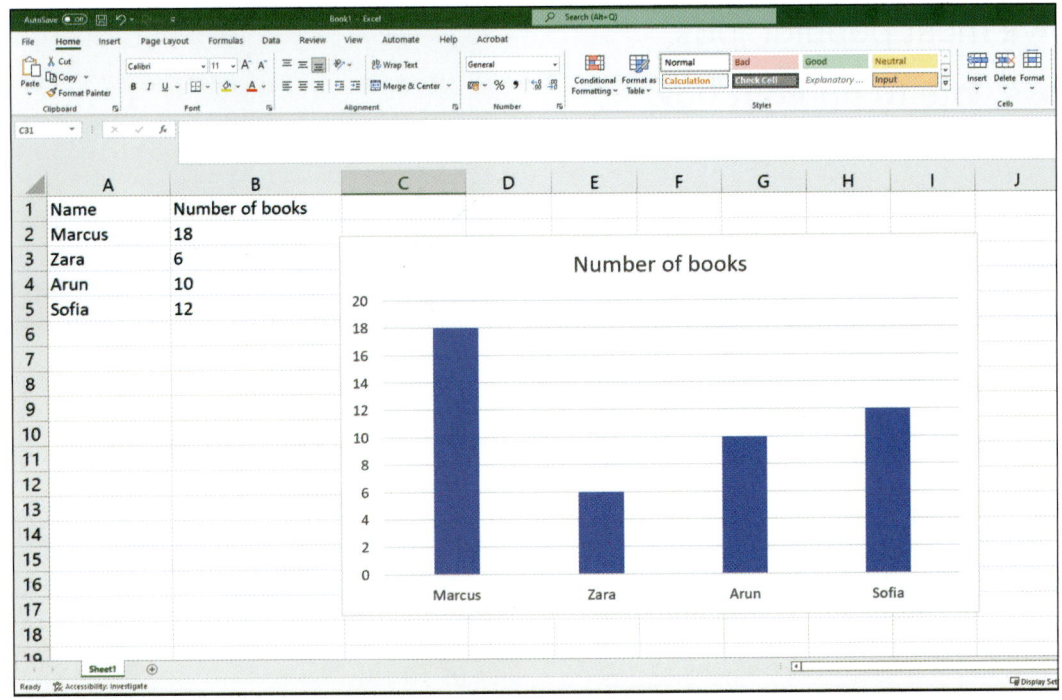

133

2 Managing data

Questions

Look at the bar chart Zara created.

4 Who read the most books?

5 Who read the fewest books?

6 Who read 10 books?

Now you will learn how to make your own bar chart.

Practical task 3

Making a bar chart from your own data

> **You will need:**
> a desktop computer, laptop or tablet, a spreadsheet program (for example, Microsoft Excel), a pencil and paper or a whiteboard pen and mini whiteboard

First, collect your data.

Have a quick discussion as a class about which jobs everyone would like to do when they're older.

Decide on the five most popular jobs.

Next, hold a class vote to find out how many people would like to do each job.

Your teacher will write the results in a table on the board.

Now make a new spreadsheet and enter this data.

Format the headings to make them stand out.

Once you have entered the data, use your spreadsheet to create a bar chart to present the data.

2.2 Super spreadsheets

Continued

You can do this in four steps:

Step 1: Select the jobs and numbers of learners by clicking, holding and dragging your pointer across the table.

Step 2: Click the 'Insert' tab.

Then click the small icon of a bar chart.

This is labelled as a 'column' chart in most spreadsheet programs.

Step 3: Choose the first option, which is a bar chart.

It is called a 'Clustered Column' chart in some spreadsheet programs.

Your bar chart will be created in your spreadsheet.

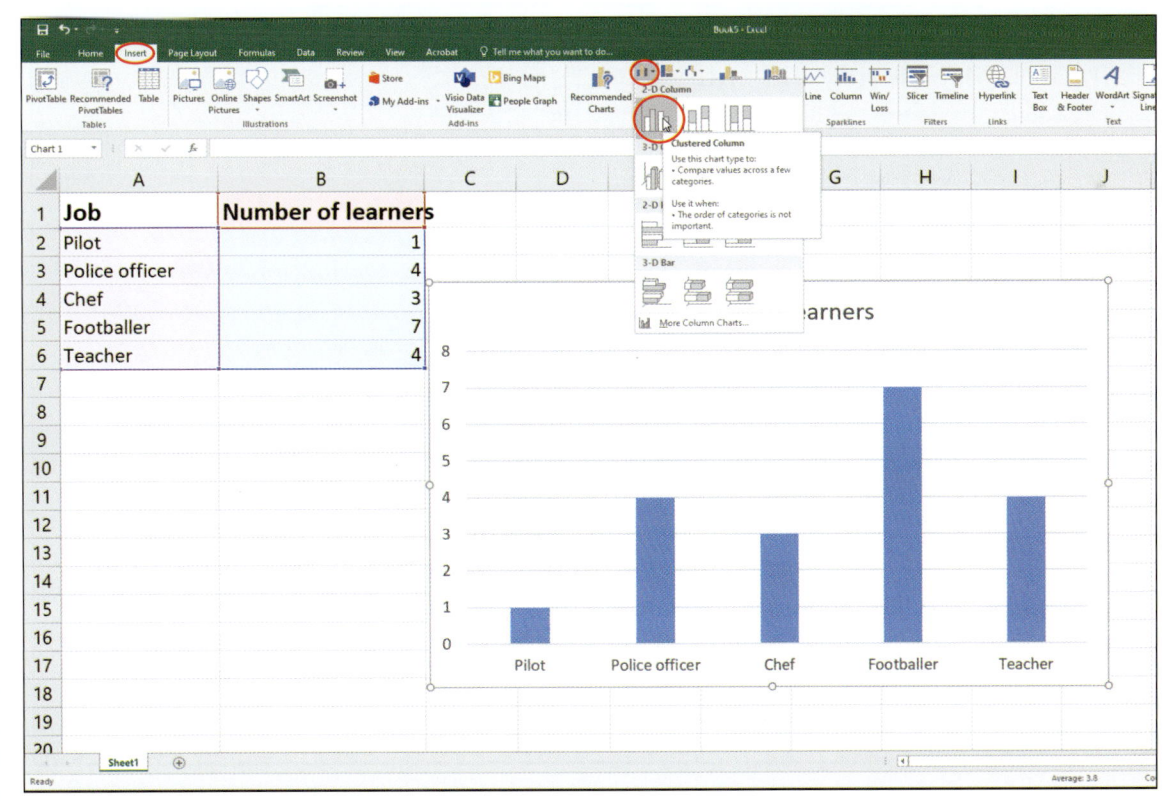

2   Managing data

Continued

Step 4: Add titles to the axes.

Axes are two lines around the graph that measure the data.

In this graph, one axis goes from bottom to top (the numbers) and one axis goes from left to right (the jobs).

To add titles, click on the '+' at the top right of the graph.

Then click on 'Axis Titles'. The words 'Axis Title' will appear in two boxes.

You can click on them to change the words.

You can match your two table headings: 'Job' and 'Number of learners'.

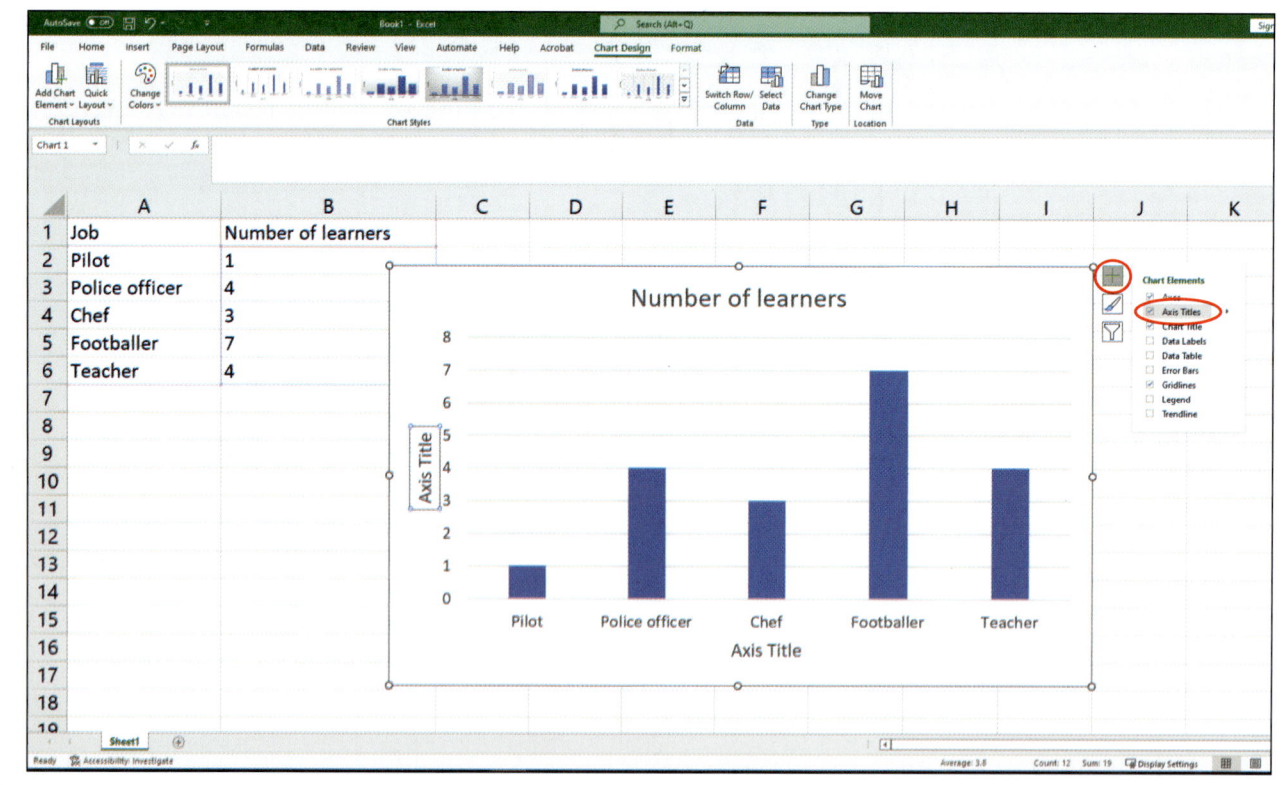

2.2 Super spreadsheets

> **Continued**
>
> **Step 5:** Finally, change the title of the graph. Click on the title that the spreadsheet program has given it and add a new title.
>
> You could call this graph 'Popular jobs'.

In this topic, you have presented data as charts. Why do you think seeing data as a chart makes it easier to understand?

Look what I can do!

- ☐ I know that spreadsheets are made from rows and columns.
- ☐ I can enter data into cells in spreadsheets.
- ☐ I can use a spreadsheet to record and represent data.
- ☐ I can format cells in spreadsheets.

2 Managing data

Project

Let's solve a problem at school

You will need:
a desktop computer, laptop or tablet, a spreadsheet program (for example, Microsoft Excel), a pencil and paper or a whiteboard pen and mini whiteboard

You will use the knowledge you have developed in this unit to solve (answer, or fix) a problem.

You will work in a group to do this.

First, you will decide on the problem you will solve.

Then you will collect data, enter it into a spreadsheet and present it using a bar chart.

Finally, you can use your data to help you solve the problem.

> Remember to check that the people you ask are happy to share their data with you.

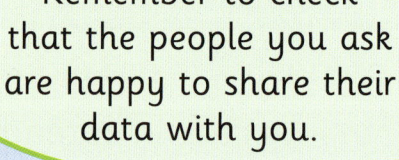

Step 1: As a group, discuss what problem you could solve by collecting data.

Your teacher will help you with this. You could:

- solve the problem of which art supplies the school should buy by finding out the most popular art activity
- solve the problem of having lots of food waste at lunchtime by finding out learners' least favourite meal.

> Remember to think carefully about which question you will ask to collect your data.

2.2 Super spreadsheets

Continued

Step 2: Decide on five possible choices that people might vote for in answer to your question.

Remember to choose things that you think a lot of people will vote for.

As a group, ask your class the question and give them the choices.

Then collect the data you need to solve your problem. Record this in a table.

Step 3: Now put this data into a new spreadsheet.

You can also format the spreadsheet to make it easier to read.

Step 4: Present your data using a bar chart.

Step 5: Use this bar chart to solve the problem.

Share your answer with your teacher.

2 Managing data

Check your progress

1 Which **two** of these problems could be solved by collecting data?

   A choosing which biscuits to buy for a party

   B creating a cake for a party

   C deciding which games to play at a party

2 What data would you collect to help solve the problems you chose in question 1?

3 Write the name of each coloured cell in this spreadsheet.

4 Which of these are types of formatting that can be used on data in cells?

   Choose **two** correct answers.

   A using the data to create a bar chart

   B making the data appear in a familiar date format

   C making the data appear as a currency with $

Continued

5 Why do we present data using charts?

   A They look colourful.

   B They make data easier and quicker to understand.

   C They tell us the best questions to ask to collect data.

6 What is the name of this way of presenting data?

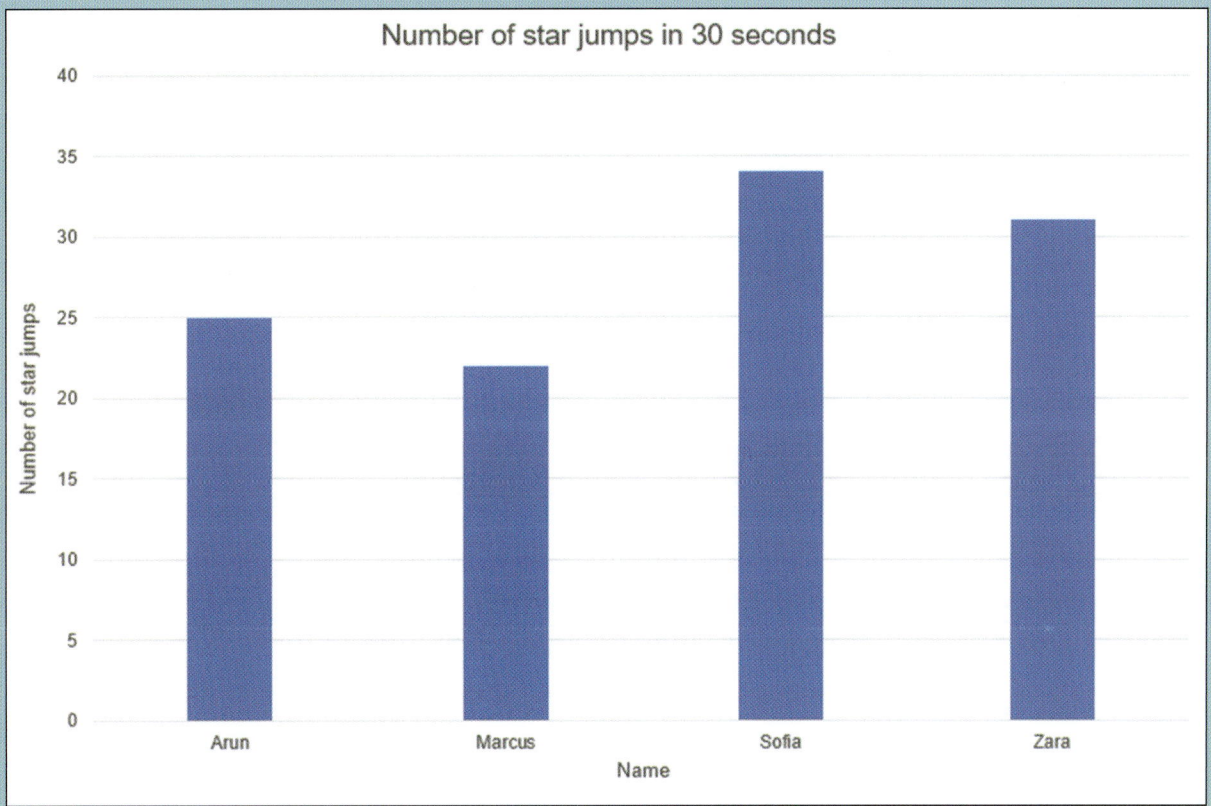

   A block graph   B pictogram   C bar chart

7 Answer the following questions about the data in question 6.

   a Who did the most star jumps?

   b Who did the fewest star jumps?

   c Who did 25 star jumps?

3 Networks and digital communication

> 3.1 Networks everywhere!

We are going to:

- find networked hardware at home and at school
- find out what we can do using networks
- understand the good and bad points of using networks.

antennas
file
internet
local area network
search engine
server
services
web browser
wi-fi access point
World Wide Web

Getting started

What do you already know?

- Digital devices can connect to a network using wires or a wireless connection (wi-fi).
- Computers can share information when they are connected to a network.
- There are risks when connecting to a network, such as your computer getting a virus.

3.1 Networks everywhere!

> **Continued**
>
> **Now try this!**
>
> Think of a time you have used a computer network.
>
> Draw a picture of yourself using it.
>
> Show what type of computer you were using and what you did on the network.
>
> Describe your picture to a partner. Listen to them describe theirs.

Wired and wireless networks

You already know that digital devices can connect to a network using wires or wi-fi.

If a digital device uses wires, it will connect using a network cable like this:

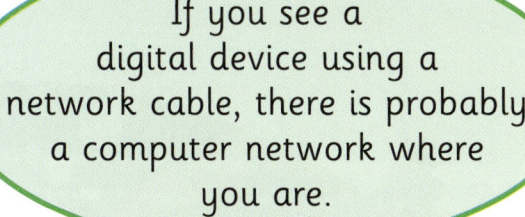

If you see a digital device using a network cable, there is probably a computer network where you are.

3 Networks and digital communication

You may have seen a digital device that looks similar to the one below either at home or in school.

If you see a digital device like this, there is probably a computer network where you are.

One job of a digital device like this is to act as a **wi-fi access point**.

Wi-fi access points let digital devices connect to a network using a wireless connection.

The wi-fi access point is connected to the network.

It lets digital devices send information to the network or receive information from it wirelessly.

These digital devices often have **antennas**.

Antennas are small poles that send and receive information.

This butterfly also has antennas, which it uses to get information.

3.1 Networks everywhere!

Unplugged activity 1

Be a network detective

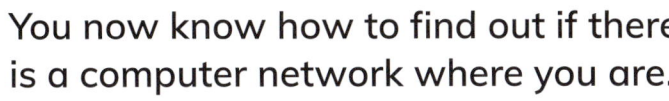

You will need:
a pencil and paper or a whiteboard pen and mini whiteboard

Detectives are people who find things out.

You now know how to find out if there is a computer network where you are.

Over the next week, see if you can find any network cables or wi-fi access points at home or in school.

If you see one, write down where you were and what you saw.

Make a class list of everywhere you found computer networks.

Does it surprise you how many places have computer networks?

Discuss as a class why these places might have computer networks.

We will learn more about how we can use networks next.

Stay safe!

Do not touch the equipment you are looking for as you may receive an electrical shock.

3 Networks and digital communication

Why have a network?

Networks let computers share information.

They can also share **services** provided by other digital devices on the network.

A service is something another digital device can do.

We can see that a printer provides the service of printing.

If a school did not have a network, each computer would need its own printer.

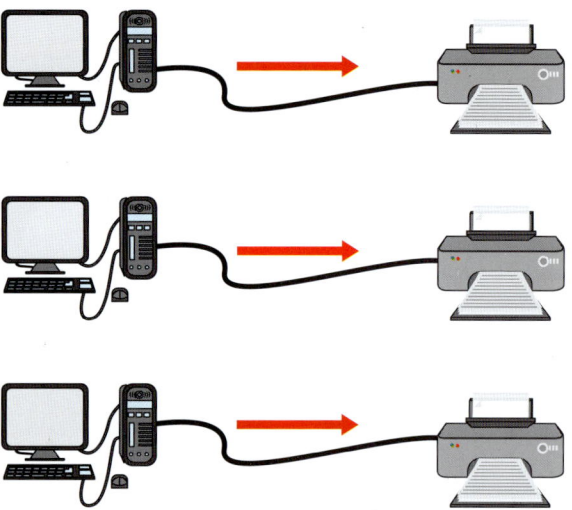

But if a school has a network, all the computers can print using the same printer.

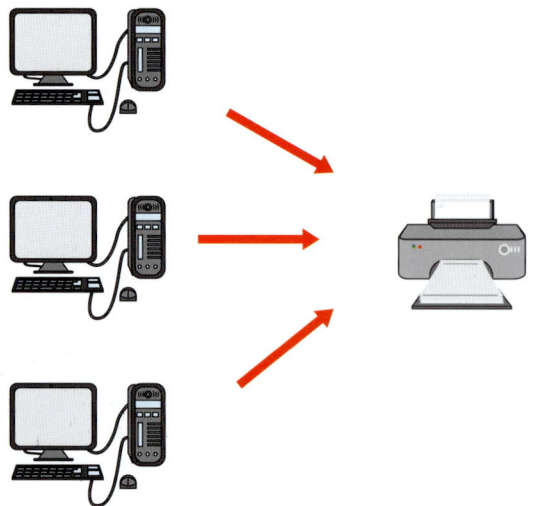

3.1 Networks everywhere!

Question

1 Discuss with a partner.

What are the advantages (good points) to a school using a printer on a network?

Local area networks (LANs)

Small networks that are in one building like a school are called **local area networks**.

Zara is at school. She is writing a story.

She could save it on the computer she is working on.

If she does this, she can only open her story on the same computer.

But if Zara saves her story on the network, she can open it on any computer that is connected to the network.

Zara decides to save her story on the network.

Her story is a **file**. This is the name we give to saved information that we can open on a computer.

Zara's file is saved to a central computer on a local area network.

The central computer is called a **server**.

This means Zara can open her file from any of the computers on the network.

147

3 Networks and digital communication

Marcus has thought of why it might be useful for a school to have a network. Discuss with a partner. Do you agree with him?

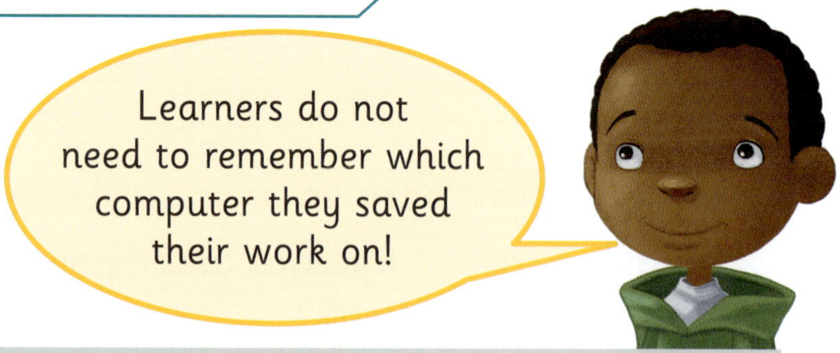

Learners do not need to remember which computer they saved their work on!

Question

2 Discuss with a partner. Can you think of any other reasons it might be useful to have a network at school?

You usually have to log in to a network using a username and password.

This is to help keep the network safe. It means you can only access your own files.

Stay safe!

It is important to keep your password for logging in to a network private to stop other people accessing your files.

3.1 Networks everywhere!

Activity 2

Is it connected to a local area network?

> You will need:
> a whiteboard pen and whiteboard, three different computers

You will work as a class with your teacher.

You will have three computers, such as a desktop computer, laptop or tablet from your classroom.

Look at the table below.

Try each of the tests in the table for each computer and complete the table as a class.

This will help you to decide if the computer is connected to a network.

Computer	Do we need to log in to use it?	Can we print from a printer not connected to the computer with a wire?	Can we open files that were saved on a different computer?	Do we think this computer is on a local area network?

Most computers are networked these days. You might find it difficult to find a computer that is not connected to a network.

149

3 Networks and digital communication

Accessing the World Wide Web

Some networks cover larger areas than local area networks.

They connect computers across different buildings or even across different countries.

The largest network of all is called the **internet**.

The internet connects computers all across the world.

Most local area networks also connect to the internet.

The internet provides lots of services.

One of these services is access to the **World Wide Web**.

The World Wide Web is information, including words, pictures and videos.

This information is organised as websites, which are made up of individual web pages.

A website about sports might have a home page with information about lots of different sports.

150

3.1 Networks everywhere!

Then it might have individual pages with more detail about each sport.

If our computer is connected to the internet, we can access these web pages to see the information.

We use a program called a **web browser** to look at things on the World Wide Web.

Examples of browsers include:

- Google Chrome
- Apple Safari
- Microsoft Edge
- Mozilla Firefox.

A **search engine** is different to a browser. Search engines let you find information on the World Wide Web. Some examples of search engines are: Google, Bing or Yahoo. Web browsers are the programs that you use to visit a search engine.

151

3 Networks and digital communication

Did you know?

Information travels through the internet as pulses of light or electricity.

A pulse is when something switches on and off quickly.

These pulses are turned back into information when they reach our computer.

Unplugged activity 3

Which websites?

> You will need:
> a pencil and paper or a whiteboard pen and mini whiteboard

Think about the websites you use most often at home.

List the three websites you use most often.

Compare your answers with a partner. Do you use the same websites?

Make a class list. Which is the most popular website?

Think of the things you can learn using the World Wide Web. How does using the World Wide Web help you to learn?

3.1 Networks everywhere!

Advantages and disadvantages of networks

Marcus said before that it would be useful having a network in school so learners did not have to remember which computer they saved their work on.

This is one advantage of having a network.

Remember, advantages are good points, so disadvantages are bad points.

You discussed some other advantages of using a network.

You might have said:

- If one networked computer breaks, you can still access your work on another computer.
- If work is saved to a network, you do not have to use the same computer each time. This means that it is not a problem if someone else is using that computer the next day.
- Other people, like teachers, can view your work when it is saved to a network.

153

3 Networks and digital communication

There are also disadvantages (bad points) of using a network.

You have already learnt that computer viruses can spread across computer networks.

These viruses can cause a lot of damage to a whole computer network.

The virus might steal private information or stop all the computers from working properly.

Remember when you discussed the advantages of a school using a printer on a network?

You might have said that having to buy just one printer saves the school money.

But there are also some disadvantages. Zara has thought of one.

> Having a network with just one printer is a disadvantage because no one can print if that printer breaks.

Do you think that having a printer on a network has more advantages or disadvantages? Why?

154

3.1 Networks everywhere!

Unplugged activity 4

Advantages and disadvantages of networks

> You will need:
> a pencil and paper or a whiteboard pen and mini whiteboard

There are a number of statements below about networks.

Write down the number of each statement, then draw:

- a tick ✓ next to the statement if it is an advantage
- a cross ✗ next to the statement if it is a disadvantage.

1 Having a network saves money because people can share digital devices like printers.

2 If the server breaks, no one can open their files.

3 It is easy to have spare copies of files as they are all stored in the server.

4 Files can be easily shared between computers.

5 Buying the cables and special equipment to build a network can be expensive.

6 Viruses can spread between computers more easily.

7 Large networks need an expert to look after them, which costs money.

How am I doing?

Find a partner and compare your answers.

Are they the same? Discuss any that are different.

3 Networks and digital communication

Look what I can do!

- ☐ I can find networked hardware at home and at school.
- ☐ I know what services are available on networks, such as accessing files, printing and accessing the World Wide Web.
- ☐ I understand the advantages and disadvantages of networks.

3.2 Secret ciphers

We are going to:
- learn what a cipher is
- understand how a cipher can keep information secret
- find out how to write and decode messages with a simple cipher.

**algorithm
cipher
decode**

Getting started

What do you already know?
- It is important to keep passwords secret.
- You should not share private information online or with people you do not know.

Now try this!

Look at the sentence below. It does not make sense!

> Secret information keeping about is topic this.

That is because it has been written in a way to disguise (hide) what it says.

Can you work out what it says?

Tell a partner what the sentence says.

Explain what you had to do to read the sentence correctly.

Starting at the end might help!

3 Networks and digital communication

Introducing ciphers

Marcus has given Zara a piece of paper which just has some numbers on it.

The numbers are:

9   1 13   1   3 15 4 5   2 18 5 1 11 5 18

Zara does not know what the numbers mean.

If we want to keep information secret, we can disguise it using a **cipher** (say *sigh-fer*).

A cipher is a type of algorithm.

Ciphers are used to keep digital information secret.

But if we know the cipher, we can **decode** the information.

This means that we can understand the meaning of it.

Remember that an algorithm is a precise set of instructions.

158

3.2 Secret ciphers

If Zara can work out the cipher, she can decode the information.

I will give you a clue. Each letter has been turned into a number.

Ah! So the gaps between the numbers show me when to start a new word.

Sofia and Zara are discussing which letters the numbers could be.

Perhaps the number '3' is the letter 'e' as it looks like a backwards capital 'E'?

Perhaps '1' is an 'L' as it looks similar.

Discuss as a class any ideas you have on how the cipher changed the letters to numbers.

- What letter might the number 1 be?
- What letter might the number 2 be?

Luckily, Marcus has the cipher so Sofia can decode the message.

The cipher is that you turn each letter into a number, starting with A = 1, B = 2, C = 3… all the way to Z = 26.

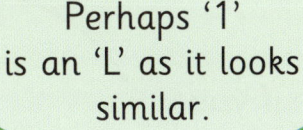

3 Networks and digital communication

Unplugged activity 1

Decoding the message

> You will need:
> a pencil and paper or a whiteboard pen and mini whiteboard,
> source file **3.1_cipher**

Use a printout of the file your teacher will give you.

Add the correct number under each letter, starting at A = 1.

You now have the cipher so you can understand Marcus's message.

To do this, look at each number in the message and write down the letter that matches it in your cipher.

The table below has the numbers that Marcus gave to Zara.

The first three numbers have been decoded for you.

Copy the table and complete it to decode the secret message.

Number	9		1	13		1	3	15	4	5		2	18	5	1	11	5	18
Letter	I		A	M														

How am I doing?

Draw a smiley face if you decoded the message.

Compare your table with a partner. Did you get the same answer?

3.2 Secret ciphers

Unplugged activity 2

Decoding secret messages

You will need:
a pencil and paper or a whiteboard pen and mini whiteboard, your completed cipher from Unplugged activity 1

I've found some more secret messages. Will you help me to decode them?

Use the cipher to decode the following messages.

Message 1:

3 9 16 8 5 18 19   11 5 5 16

9 14 6 15 18 13 1 20 9 15 14   19 5 3 18 5 20

Message 2:

20 8 5   13 5 19 19 1 7 5   9 19

23 18 9 20 20 5 14   23 9 20 8   1   3 9 16 8 5 18

3 Networks and digital communication

Continued

Message 3:

20 8 5   3 9 16 8 5 18   9 19   21 19 5 4
20 15   4 5 3 15 4 5   20 8 5   13 5 19 19 1 7 5

How am I doing?

Compare your messages with a partner.

Did you get the same answers?

Draw a tick for each message you decoded correctly.

Where are ciphers used?

Ciphers were used by armies to keep messages private.

This is the Enigma machine. It was used in the Second World War by the German army to disguise messages using a cipher so their enemies could not read them.

Today, a lot of information is sent using digital communication like email.

Many of these digital communications use ciphers to disguise the information.

This is in case someone who is not supposed to see it looks at it.

The information is decoded when it reaches the person it was meant to be sent to, so they can read it.

3.2 Secret ciphers

Arun sends a message to Sofia.

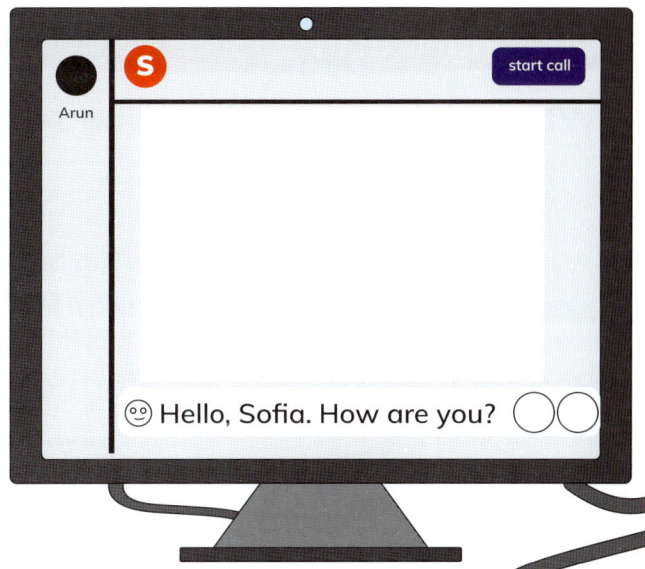

A cipher is used to disguise the information.

When Sofia opens the message, the cipher is used to decode the message.

Ciphers are also used to disguise important information kept as files on networks, such as people's usernames and passwords.

This stops anyone who gets access to a network from seeing the information.

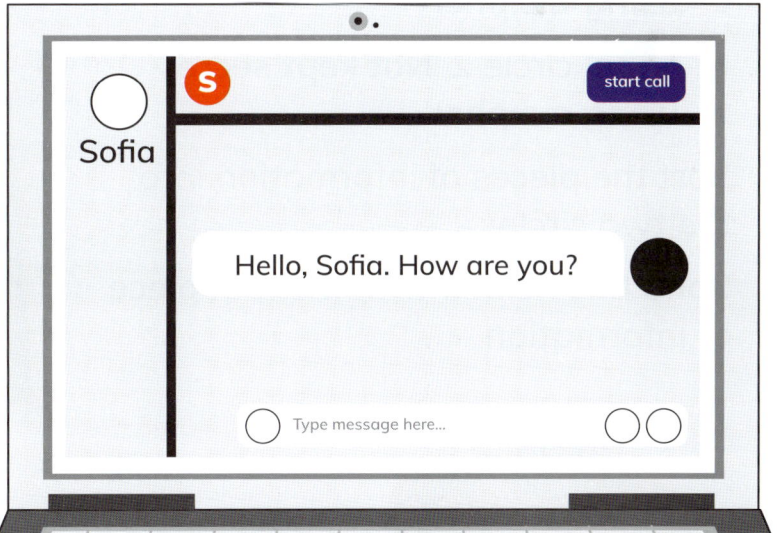

163

3 Networks and digital communication

Unplugged activity 3

Which information should be secret?

> You will need:
> a pencil and paper or a whiteboard pen and mini whiteboard, completed cipher from Unplugged activity 1

Read these examples of information.

- stories on a news website
- someone's bank details
- someone's private emails
- information about holidays from a web page
- someone's health records
- a menu for a restaurant

- Draw two circles.
- Label circle 1 '**Kept secret using a cipher**'.
- Label circle 2 '**Not kept secret using a cipher**'.

Sort the pieces of information into the two circles.

Sofia has helped with the first piece of information

I think someone's bank details would be kept secret using a cipher.

164

3.2 Secret ciphers

> **Continued**
>
> **How am I doing?**
>
> Compare your two sets of answers with a partner.
>
> Did you get the same or different answers?
>
> Discuss any answers that are different and try to decide on the correct answer.
>
> Now you can try writing some of your own secret messages!
>
> Work with a partner.
>
> Use your completed cipher to write a message to your partner.
>
> When you have written your message, swap and decode them to read what they say.

How safe is the cipher?

There are many different types of cipher.

Some ciphers are easy to guess or work out.

You might have guessed how the A1Z26 cipher worked at the start of this topic.

A cipher that is easy to guess is not very safe. Someone could decode your information without being given the cipher.

Some ciphers use complicated mathematics to make them very safe.

Let's have a go at making our own cipher.

3 Networks and digital communication

Unplugged activity 4

Make and use your own cipher

> **You will need:**
> a pencil and paper or a whiteboard pen and mini whiteboard,
> source file **3.1_cipher** (the original file – not your completed cipher)

Use a printout of the file your teacher gives you.

Add the numbers 1–26 beneath the letters.

They can be in any order you choose, but they should not be the same as the A1Z26 cipher, so they should not start with A = 1 and end with Z = 26.

Use your cipher to write a message to a partner.

Give your message to your partner.

Can they decode it without the cipher? They probably can't!

Now give them the cipher so they can decode the message.

3.2 Secret ciphers

> **Stay safe!**
>
> If a website is using a cipher to disguise information, it will show a small closed padlock in the address bar: 🔒
>
> This helps you to know the information you enter will be safe.
>
> It does not mean the whole website is real or safe, so always ask an adult if you are unsure.

Think about what skills you used in this topic.
You had to be precise when you followed the ciphers. What other skills did you use?

Look what I can do!

- [ ] I know that a cipher keeps information secret.
- [ ] I know what types of information are kept secret by ciphers.
- [ ] I can decode a message using a simple cipher.
- [ ] I can write a message using a simple cipher.

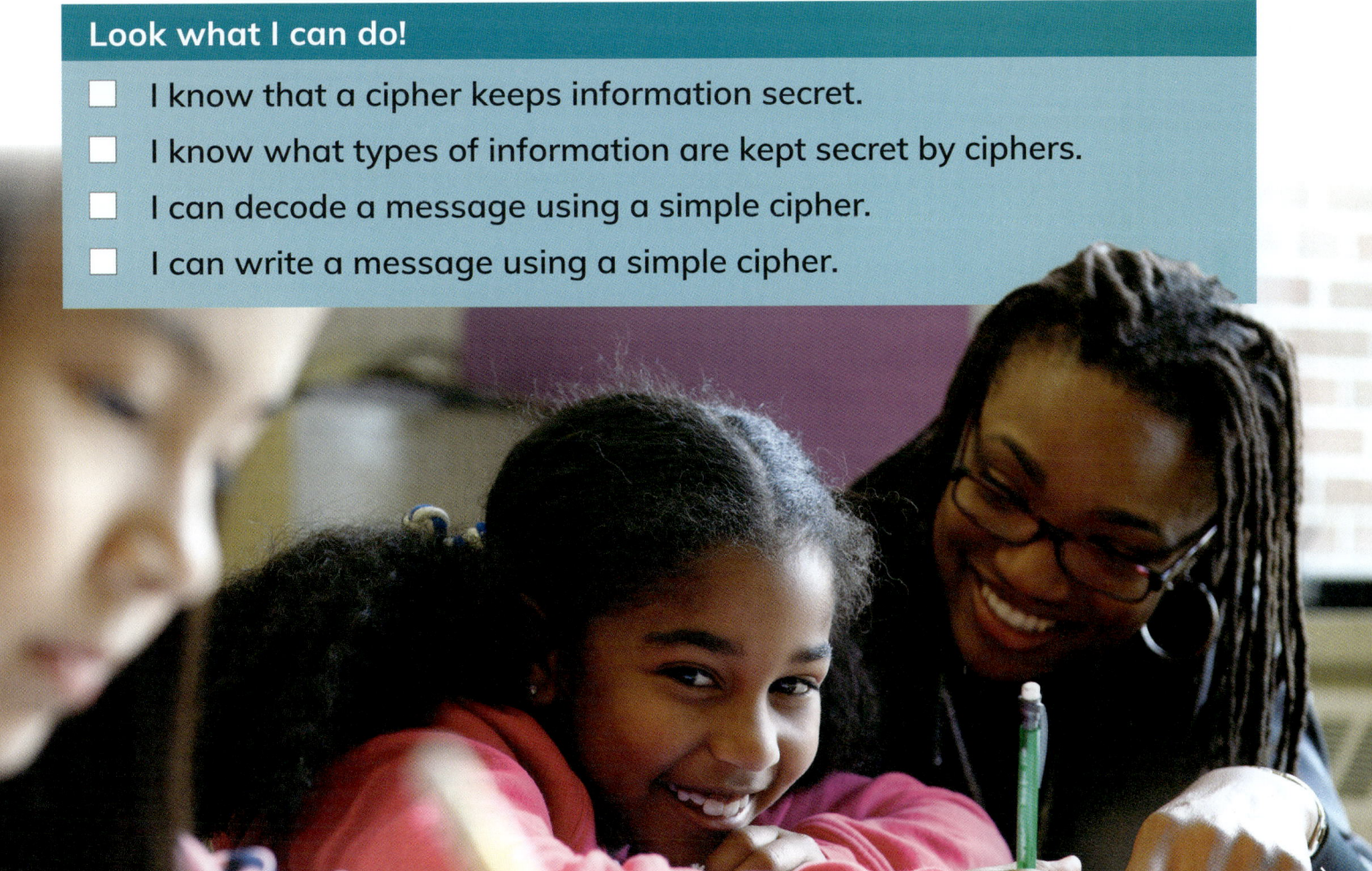

3 Networks and digital communication

Project

Make a poster for a home network

> You will need:
> a pencil and paper, colouring pencils or pens, source file **3.1_cipher** (the original file – not your completed cipher)

This project is in two parts.

First, you will make a poster with a design for a local area network for your home.

Next, you will create a cipher to disguise information on your network.

Part 1: Poster with local area network design

Start your poster by drawing a local area network for your home.

It should say which digital devices and services will be included in the network.

You can choose:

- which computers will be connected to it (such as tablets, laptops, desktop computers) and the location of these (such as the living room, study, kitchen)
- whether it has a printer connected to it
- whether it has a connection to the internet for accessing the World Wide Web.

Next, add three advantages (good points) of having this network.

Part 2: Cipher design

Now make your own cipher to disguise information on your network and keep it safe.

You can use source file **3.1_cipher** to help you.

Write your name on your poster using your cipher to disguise it.

3.2 Secret ciphers

Check your progress

1 What is this called?

  A network cable   B input   C wi-fi

2 Arun and Zara are discussing printing their work.

  They are using their school's local area network, which has a printer on it.

  Who is correct?

> I can't print because there isn't a printer connected to my computer with a wire.

> You can use that printer because it is connected to the school network.

3 Networks and digital communication

Continued

3 What information is available on the World Wide Web?

   A only words

   B only pictures and videos

   C words, pictures and videos

4 Which of these is a disadvantage (bad point) of a local area network?

   A Files are easy to back up as they are all stored in a central special computer.

   B Programs are cheaper to buy for networked computers.

   C If the central computer that stores the files breaks, nobody can access any of their files.

5 What is a cipher?

   A a type of information

   B an algorithm for writing information to keep it secret

   C a file saved on a computer network

6 Use the A1Z26 cipher to work out what this coded message says.

Cipher												
A	B	C	D	E	F	G	H	I	J	K	L	M
1	2	3	4	5	6	7	8	9	10	11	12	13
N	O	P	Q	R	S	T	U	V	W	X	Y	Z
14	15	16	17	18	19	20	21	22	23	24	25	26

Message:

23 5   14 5 5 4   20 8 5   3 9 16 8 5 18   20 15
4 5 3 15 4 5   20 8 9 19

4 Computer systems

> 4.1 Hardware and software working together

We are going to:
- compare the different jobs that hardware and software do
- learn that files can be stored on a computer
- look at different types of files.

app   hardware
computer system   icon
download   software
hard drive

Getting started

What do you already know?

- Hardware is the parts of a computer system that we can see or touch.
- A computer system is a computer and all the hardware connected to it.
- Software helps the computer system to do its job.
- The programs that computers use are called software.
- Software sends messages between the hardware and different parts of the computer.

4 Computer systems

Continued

Now try this!

You already know about programs and apps (application software), which we use on computers.

With a partner, make a list of five apps you have used.

You could think about anything you like to play or use on a smartphone or tablet, such as games.

Next to the name of each app, write a sentence about what it is used for.

Hardware and software

Remember that **hardware** is the parts of a computer system that we can see or touch.

My laptop has a screen, a keyboard and a touchpad. I also have a printer. These are all pieces of hardware.

172

4.1 Hardware and software working together

Find a **computer system** in your school.

Remember, a computer system is a computer and all the hardware connected to it.

What hardware can you see?

Look around the room. Is there any other hardware?

Software is the programs that computers use.

Software tells a computer what to do.

You cannot see or touch software.

On some digital devices, pieces of software are called applications, or **apps** for short.

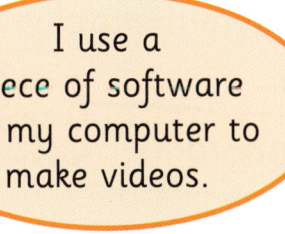

I use a piece of software on my computer to make videos.

Questions

1. Name three pieces of software on a computer you use at home or at school.
2. What is the name of your favourite software for typing things like stories or letters?
3. What other words can we use instead of 'software'?

Without software, the computer would not be very useful.

Imagine trying to do some digital painting without a painting program!

4 Computer systems

Unplugged activity 1

Is it hardware or software?

> You will need:
> a pencil and paper or a whiteboard pen and mini whiteboard

Look at the words below. They are all parts of a computer system.

Are they hardware or software?

Copy and complete the table.

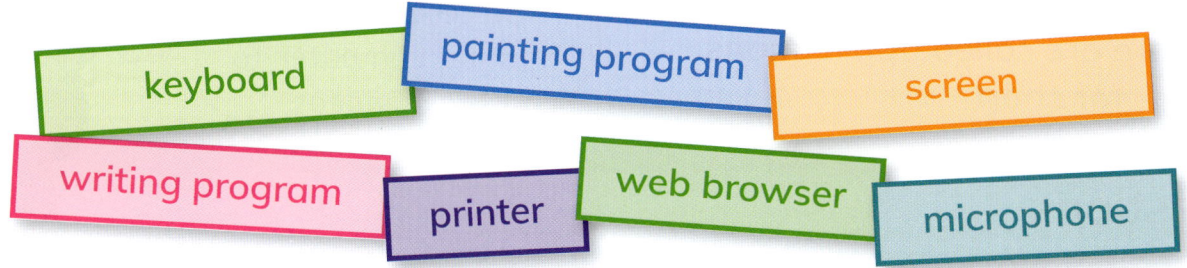

Hardware	Software

4.1 Hardware and software working together

Now that you know the difference between hardware and software, you are going to think about what they can be used for.

Unplugged activity 2

What am I describing?

Marcus, Sofia, Arun and Zara are playing a game.

One person describes something and the other person has to guess what it is.

What are they describing?

It is a piece of hardware. When you play a song from your computer, the sound comes out of it.

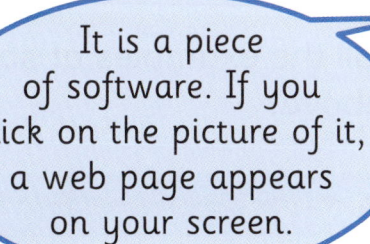

It is a piece of software. If you click on the picture of it, a web page appears on your screen.

It is a piece of hardware. You look at it to see your work.

It is a piece of software. You use this to write on the computer.

175

4 Computer systems

Parts of a computer system

The hardware and software need to work together so the computer system works properly.

Each part of the system has its own job to do.

Here is a description of how hardware and software work together:

> We use a keyboard to type the letter 'a' into a writing program.
>
> The computer follows the instruction.
>
> The instruction is then sent back to the writing program and shown on your screen as a letter 'a'.

Questions

4 Can you list all the examples of hardware from the description above?

5 Can you list all the examples of software from the description above?

Unplugged activity 3

What do hardware and software do?

You will need:
a pencil and paper or a whiteboard pen and mini whiteboard

Copy and complete the table below to show some of the parts of a computer system and the jobs they do.

In the last row, choose your own piece of software to add.

This might be software that you use to type, play games or make presentations.

4.1 Hardware and software working together

Continued

Name	Is it hardware or software?	What does it do?
keyboard		
writing program		
	hardware	It moves a pointer around the screen and is used to choose things.
web browser		
microphone		
	hardware	It prints out work.
	software	

How am I doing?

Compare the answers in your table with a partner.

Were they the same or different?

Talk about the differences. Explain your choices.

177

4 Computer systems

Downloading

We can download more software to add it to a computer.

You have downloaded programs to your computer before.

> Remember, download means to move information from one computer to another computer, often using the internet.

In Topic 1.6, you downloaded programs onto a micro:bit.

You can also download programs that help you make music or edit photos.

Sometimes you have to pay for things you download and sometimes they are free.

> **Stay safe!**
>
> Ask an adult before you download any programs.
>
> Programs should only be downloaded from trusted places, like a proper app store.

File types

We can store information in a file in a computer system.

Files can store:

- text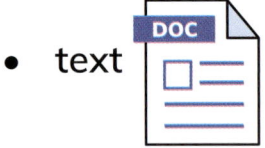
- pictures
- music
- videos

You can see that each type of file has a different icon.

178

4.1 Hardware and software working together

Activity 4

Finding files

> You will need:
> a desktop computer or laptop

Look on your computer.

Open the documents or downloads section.

Can you see any files saved there?

What is one of the files called?

What different file types can you see?

Now that you have looked at the files on your own computer, let's have a look at the files on Marcus's computer.

Unplugged activity 5

Name that file type!

> You will need:
> a pencil and paper or a whiteboard pen and mini whiteboard

The picture below shows all the files stored on Marcus's computer.

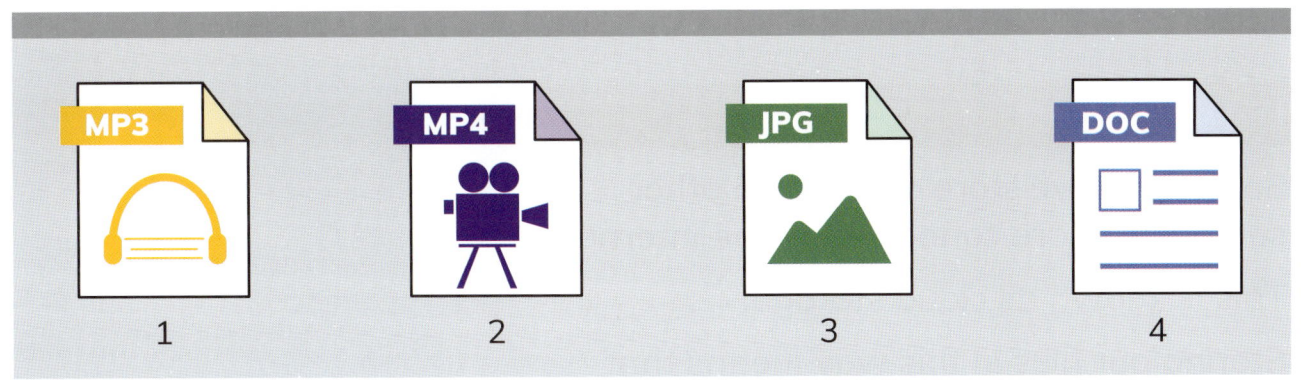

179

4 Computer systems

Continued

Match the icons to the correct file names.

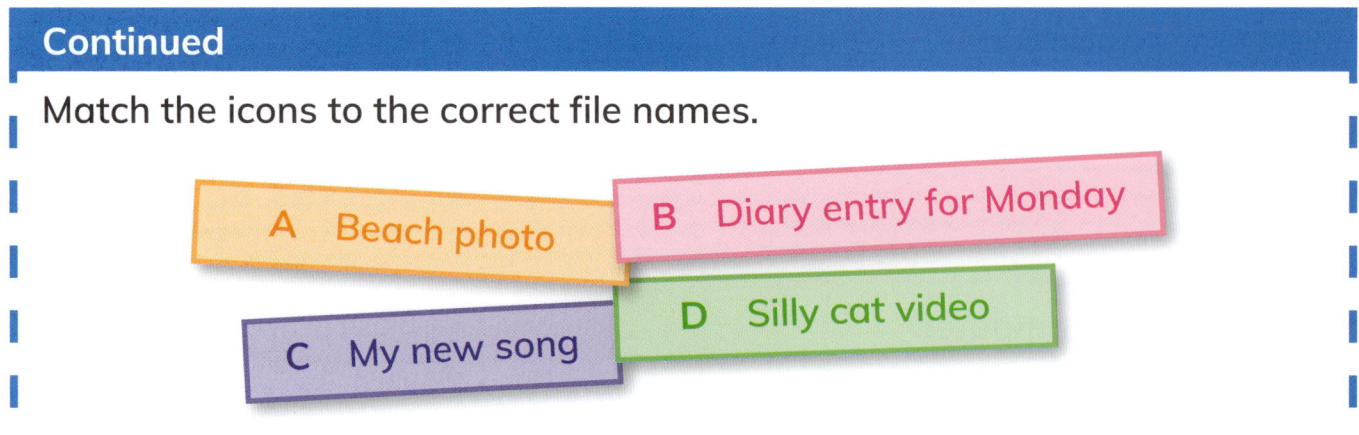

A Beach photo

B Diary entry for Monday

C My new song

D Silly cat video

Storing files

A computer keeps files on its **hard drive**.

The hard drive is the part of a computer where data is stored.

If we save our data on a computer's hard drive, we need to go back to the same computer to find our files.

If we have lots of videos or pictures stored on our computer's hard drive, it might fill up.

Once it is full, we have to delete some files or use another hard drive.

Did you know?

Sometimes we store our files on other servers that are connected to the internet.

This is known as cloud storage.

Storing our files in this way means that we can access them from any computer that is connected to the internet.

180

4.1 Hardware and software working together

If we store our files in an organised way on a computer, it makes them easy to find.

How do you keep your work organised at school or home?

Is it easier to learn if you are organised?

Look what I can do!

- ☐ I know about the different jobs that hardware and software do.
- ☐ I can find files that are stored on a computer.
- ☐ I can recognise different types of files.

4 Computer systems

> 4.2 The role of robots

We are going to:
- learn how computers can control machines all around us
- find out how robots help us in the real world
- learn why robots are used in factories.

Getting started

factory   program
machine   robot
motion sensor   sensor

What do you already know?
- Robots are built to do certain jobs without lots of help from humans.
- Robots collect information.
- They use this information to help them do their job.
- Robots often have moving parts which also help them do their job.

4.2 The role of robots

> **Continued**
>
> **Now try this!**
>
> Look at these pictures of robots at work.
>
> For each picture, write down the job that you think the robot is doing.
>
> 1
>
> 2
>
> 3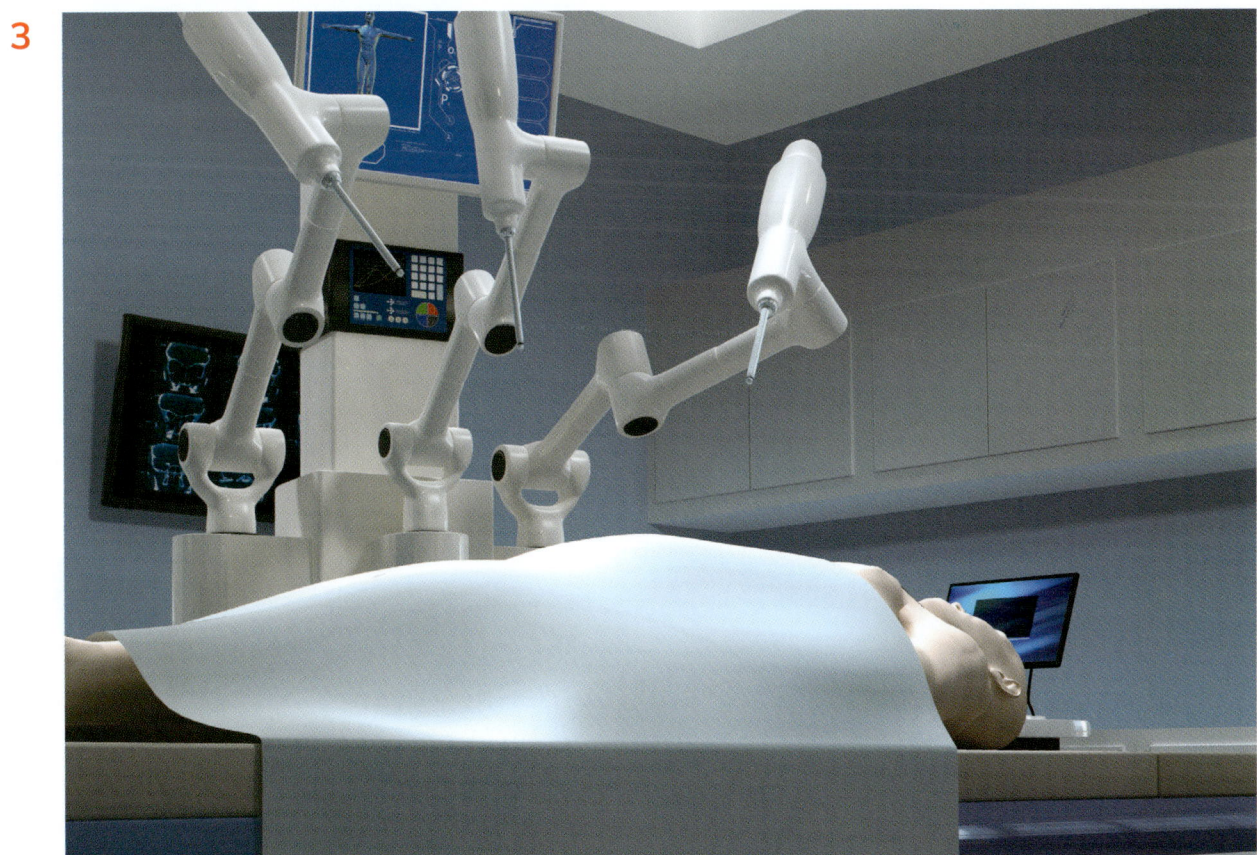
>
> Discuss your answers with a partner.

4 Computer systems

Programming all around us

You already know that a computer program is a set of instructions that a computer can understand.

We will learn about how computers can be programmed to control things like **robots** later.

Remember, robots are digital devices that can do jobs without much help from humans.

First, we will look at some more familiar things.

Question

Look at this picture of a busy street.

1 Which things are programmed by a computer?

Arun has found the first one for you.

Compare your answers with a partner.

The car park barrier has been programmed by a computer. It has been programmed to lift when there is a car in front of it.

4.2 The role of robots

Now look at this photo.

These doors have a **sensor** above them.

Sensors are digital devices that check and record data around them.

These doors are controlled by a computer program.

The program checks whether there is movement (or motion) in front of the sensor.

It is called a **motion sensor**.

The same sort of sensor is used in a car park barrier.

sensor

The motion sensor acts as an input device.

Remember, an input is information.

When the motion sensor senses movement, it sends a message to the doors to open.

The doors opening is the output.

There are lots of motion sensors around us — lights that switch on when you go in a toilet, or burglar alarms that make a noise when someone goes in a room. Look out for motion sensors around you!

185

4 Computer systems

Unplugged activity 1

What is being controlled?

> You will need:
> a pencil and paper or a whiteboard pen and mini whiteboard

There are three programs below, and three things that are being controlled by the programs.

They are mixed up.

Match each program with the thing you think it is controlling.

1 If someone presses the button, change the light to green.	**A** Vending machine
2 If someone presses the button and pays the correct amount, push the item forward so it drops to the bottom.	**B** Car parking system
3 If the sensor gets too close to something, make a noise.	**C** Pedestrian crossing

4.2 The role of robots

> **Continued**
>
> **How am I doing?**
>
> Compare your answers with a partner. Were any of them more difficult to match?

Real-world robots

Sometimes robots are better at doing a task (job) than humans.

We can use robots if something is too dangerous or difficult for a human to do.

This robot is called the Mars rover. It has been built to explore the planet Mars.

Humans cannot breathe on Mars and it is very cold at night, but that is not a problem for this robot.

You already know that robots in real life often do not look like robots in books or films.

They might not have arms or faces, like humans.

They have what they need to do their job.

4 Computer systems

Factory robots

A **factory** is a place where things are made.

These things will be sold.

Most factories have a mix of humans and **machines** to do different jobs.

A machine is a device with some moving parts that uses power to do a job.

A robot is a type of machine.

Here are some reasons why robots are used in factories:

- Robots can be useful when jobs have to be repeated over and over again. Robots do not get tired or bored like humans do.
- Robots are easy to keep clean, which is important in a factory that makes food or drinks.
- Robots can be more precise than humans. This means robots are less likely to make mistakes.

> Remember, precise means clear and correct.

Question

2 This robot is in a factory.

   What do you think it is doing?

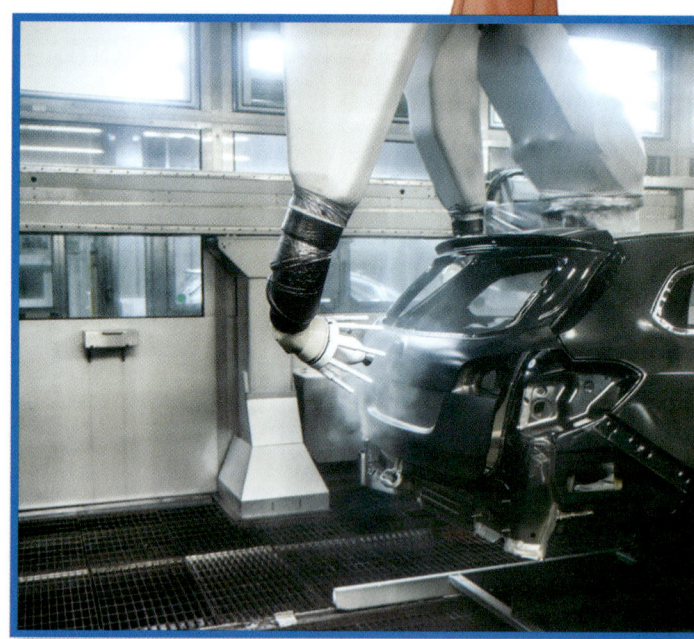

4.2 The role of robots

Unplugged activity 2

A visit to an orange juice factory

> You will need:
> a pencil and paper or a whiteboard pen and mini whiteboard

Marcus, Sofia, Arun and Zara are on a school trip.

They are at a factory where robots are used to make orange juice.

We took photos of the different robots that we saw in the factory, but we can't remember which jobs they did.

Can you help us match each photo to the robot's job?

4 Computer systems

Continued

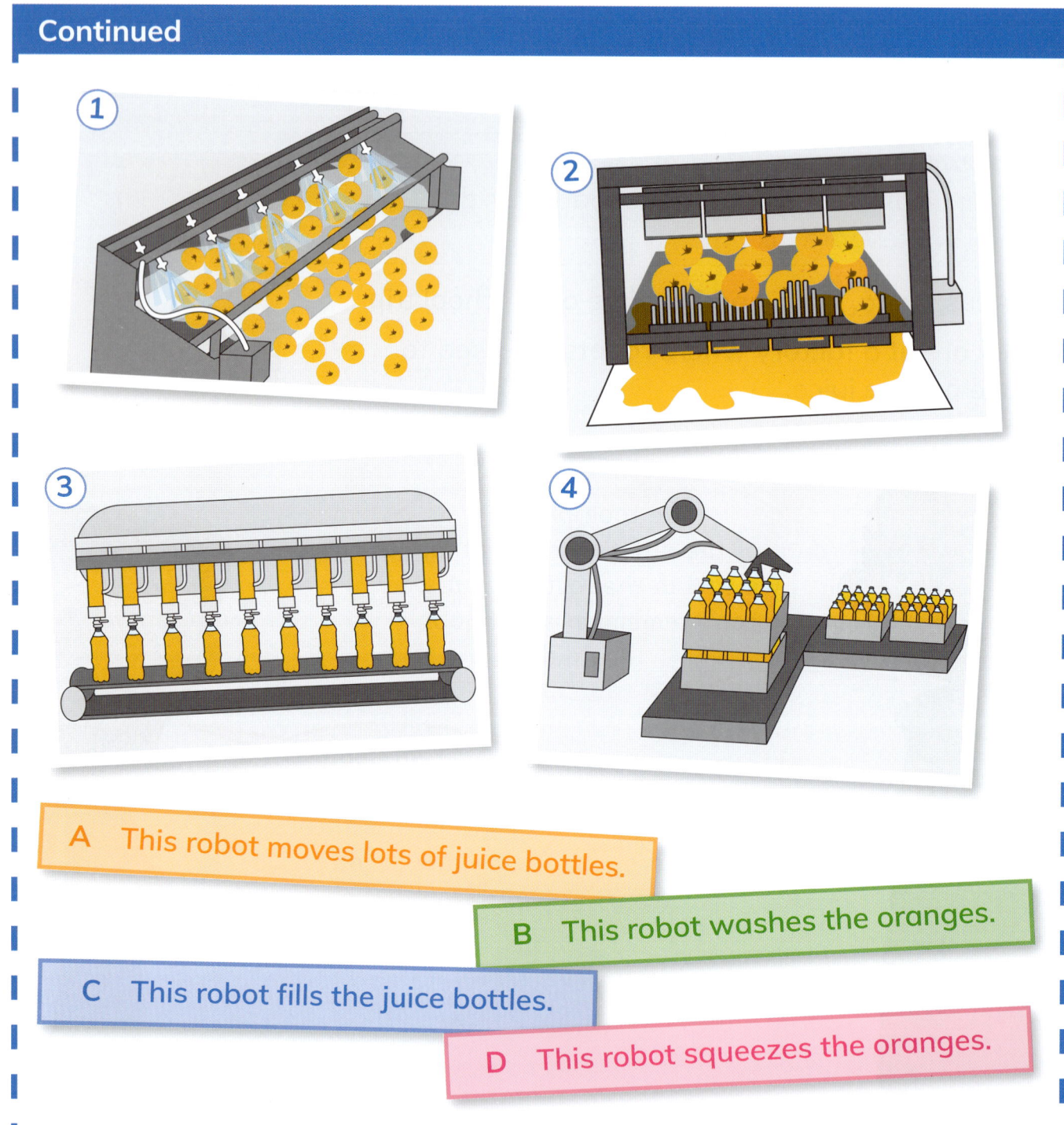

A This robot moves lots of juice bottles.

B This robot washes the oranges.

C This robot fills the juice bottles.

D This robot squeezes the oranges.

You have learnt why robots are used in factories.

You have seen some examples of robots being used in a factory.

Now you will test what you have learnt.

4.2 The role of robots

Unplugged activity 3

Why choose a robot?

> You will need:
> a pencil and paper or a whiteboard pen and mini whiteboard

Look at these tasks.

A robot is used to help with each task.

1 Packing chocolates

2 Moving large boxes

3 Counting tablets into a medicine bottle

4 Turning wheels of cheese

4 Computer systems

> **Continued**
>
> Now looks at these reasons why a robot might be better at each task than a human.
>
> A faster and more precise than humans
>
> B more hygienic (cleaner)
>
> C can lift heavy things
>
> D will not get tired
>
> Write down the photo number, then the letters to show the reasons for each photo.
>
> You can use the reasons more than once.
>
> Zara has done the first one for you.

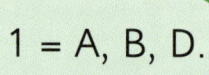

1 = A, B, D.

Why choose a human?

We have looked at lots of examples where robots can do a job better than humans.

However, jobs that involve thinking and making decisions might be better done by a human.

Humans can do things like choosing which oranges are good and bad by looking at them, or checking food to make sure it tastes nice.

Robots cannot see, touch or hear like humans can.

They can only do what they have been programmed to do.

Could I program a robot to look after me when I'm sad?

I don't think so. Robots can't understand your feelings.

4.2 The role of robots

Unplugged activity 4

True or false?

You will need:
a pencil and paper or a whiteboard pen and mini whiteboard

With a partner, look at each statement and write down whether it is **True** or **False**.

A Robots that are used in factories are expensive.

B Robots get tired.

C Robots can only do what they have been programmed to do.

D Robots get bored.

E Robots cannot smell things.

F A robot can change its own program.

G Robots can do tasks over and over again.

Did you know?

Some of the earliest robots were called automatons, which means a machine that works on its own without the need for human control.

These robots were made to entertain us, rather than to help us with a job.

Some of them could even draw and play music!

193

4 Computer systems

Robots are often programmed to repeat the same thing over and over again.

Repeating something many times can be useful when we are learning something.

Can you think of any times when you have practised something over and over again until you knew it?

Look what I can do!

☐ I know how computers can control a range of machines.

☐ I understand how robots help us in the real world.

☐ I can give examples of how robots can be used in factories.

> 4.3 Inputs and outputs around us

We are going to:

- find input devices in computer systems
- know the difference between manual and automatic input devices
- learn what the Internet of Things is.

> automatic input device
> Internet of Things
> manual input device
> sensor

Getting started

What do you already know?

- To input means to send information into a device.
- An input is information.
- To output is when a device sends out information.
- An output is what happens when a program or algorithm is followed.
- Sensors are digital devices that check and record data around them.

4 Computer systems

> **Continued**
>
> **Now try this!**
>
> You already know that devices are part of a computer system.
>
> Remember that a computer system is a computer and the hardware connected to it.
>
> Look at a digital device you like to use and make a list of any output devices you can see.

Input devices

Remember, we use input devices to send information into a computer.

Question

1 Look at the picture.

   Make a list of all the input devices you can see.

4.3 Inputs and outputs around us

Manual input devices

Most of the input devices you found in the picture are examples of **manual input devices**.

Manual means doing something with your hands.

So manual inputs are controlled by a person using their hands.

When you use a mouse, you point at things and choose them on a screen.

You control the mouse with your hand so it is a manual input.

Unplugged activity 1

How are manual input devices used?

> You will need:
> a pencil and paper or a whiteboard pen and mini whiteboard

For each of these manual input devices, write a sentence to describe how it is used by a person.

Marcus has done the first one for you.

1.

A person presses the keys to make letters appear on the screen.

2.

3.

4.

197

4 Computer systems

Automatic input devices

Some input devices do not need a person to make them work.

A person will program the digital device at first, and then the device can do its job without help from people.

These are called **automatic input devices**.

Automatic means that a machine is programmed once and then can work by itself without people.

Sensors are an example of an automatic input device.

You have already learnt about sensors.

Sensors check and record data and send it into a computer.

I wonder how streetlights know what time to come on in the evening.

They use a light sensor. When it gets darker, the sensor sends a message to the computer to turn the lights on.

Sensors can check lots of things, including:

- temperature
- light
- sound
- movement (motion).

Then sensors turn the information into data that a computer can understand.

4.3 Inputs and outputs around us

Unplugged activity 2

Input devices around us

> **You will need:**
> a pencil and paper or a whiteboard pen and mini whiteboard

Look at the input devices below.

Write down the number of each object.

Then write whether it is a manual input device (controlled by a person using their hands) or whether it has an automatic input device inside it, like a sensor (which does not need a person to make it work after it has been programmed).

1 This controls a pointer on a computer screen when someone moves it.

2 This flushes when there is movement in front of it.

3 This turns the heating on when the temperature is below a certain point.

4 This turns on when it gets dark.

4 Computer systems

> **Continued**
>
> 5 This takes a photo when someone presses a button.
>
> 6 These turn when they sense movement.
>
>
>

> **How am I doing?**
>
> Compare your answers with a partner.
>
> If your partner agrees with one of your answers, draw a smiley face.
>
> If your partner disagrees with one of your answers, discuss it and try to agree on the correct answer.

Questions

2 What is the difference between a manual input device and an automatic input device?

3 Give one example of each type of input device.

4 Why might someone want to use an automatic input device instead of a manual input device?

4.3 Inputs and outputs around us

> **Did you know?**
>
> You might have seen people use their fingerprints or faces to unlock a digital device or pay for something.
>
> These are also types of input.

Connecting digital devices to the internet

Some of the input and output devices we use can be connected to the internet.

You already know that the internet is a network of computers connected around the world.

When we take everyday things such as fridges and televisions and connect them to the internet or other digital devices, they are known as the **Internet of Things**.

These everyday things collect and share data using the internet.

The digital device in the picture lets someone control things inside their home. It can:

- control the temperature
- play music
- turn on the kettle or the oven
- lock the door.

We often use the word 'smart' in the name of an object to show that it can connect to the internet.

201

4 Computer systems

This person has a smart watch.

It can be used to pay for things in a shop by touching it on a card reader.

It uses the internet to connect to the person's bank account.

A smart watch can also check your health.

It can measure how much exercise you do.

It connects to the internet to save the data it collects and finds patterns in the data to help you get fitter.

Smart devices can also connect to other digital devices.

One way is to connect a smartphone to a speaker to play music.

The smart house

As technology develops, we are beginning to see more digital devices in the home that can connect to the internet.

Some people might have a smart:
- doorbell
- fridge
- shower
- light
- blind.

4.3 Inputs and outputs around us

We will have a closer look at a smart fridge.

When someone puts food and drinks in the fridge, the barcodes printed on those things are scanned.

This is a barcode:

The fridge stores data about what is inside it.

The fridge uses software to tell the person when the food and drink needs to be used by.

It also gives them ideas for recipes they can make with the food they have.

As the person uses the things, they are added to a shopping list so that they will not run out.

Item	Yogurt
Number	5
Use by	Friday
Recipe ideas	Smoothie

203

4 Computer systems

Unplugged activity 3

Smart devices at home

> You will need:
> a pencil and paper or a whiteboard pen and mini whiteboard

Work with a partner.

Look at the smart devices people might have at home.

Match the statements about what smart devices do with the names of the smart devices.

1. You can see who is outside your house from your phone.
2. You can check what food you have.
3. You can turn on the water with your phone to have a wash.
4. You can turn on your lights from your phone.
5. You can put your blinds up or down without touching them.
6. You can come home to a warm house by using your phone when you are out.

A smart blinds   B smart shower   C smart fridge

D smart doorbell   E smart heating   F smart lighting

4.3 Inputs and outputs around us

Activity 4

Selling a smart device

> You will need:
> a desktop computer or laptop with a keyboard and internet access,
> a pencil and paper or a whiteboard pen and mini whiteboard

Choose one of the smart devices from Unplugged activity 3.

Imagine that you have just invented this device.

Now you have to sell it to a friend.

Use the internet to find out more about your smart device.

Write down what it can do and how this makes it useful.

> My digital device is smart lighting. It turns your lights on or off. This means you don't have to walk to the light switch.

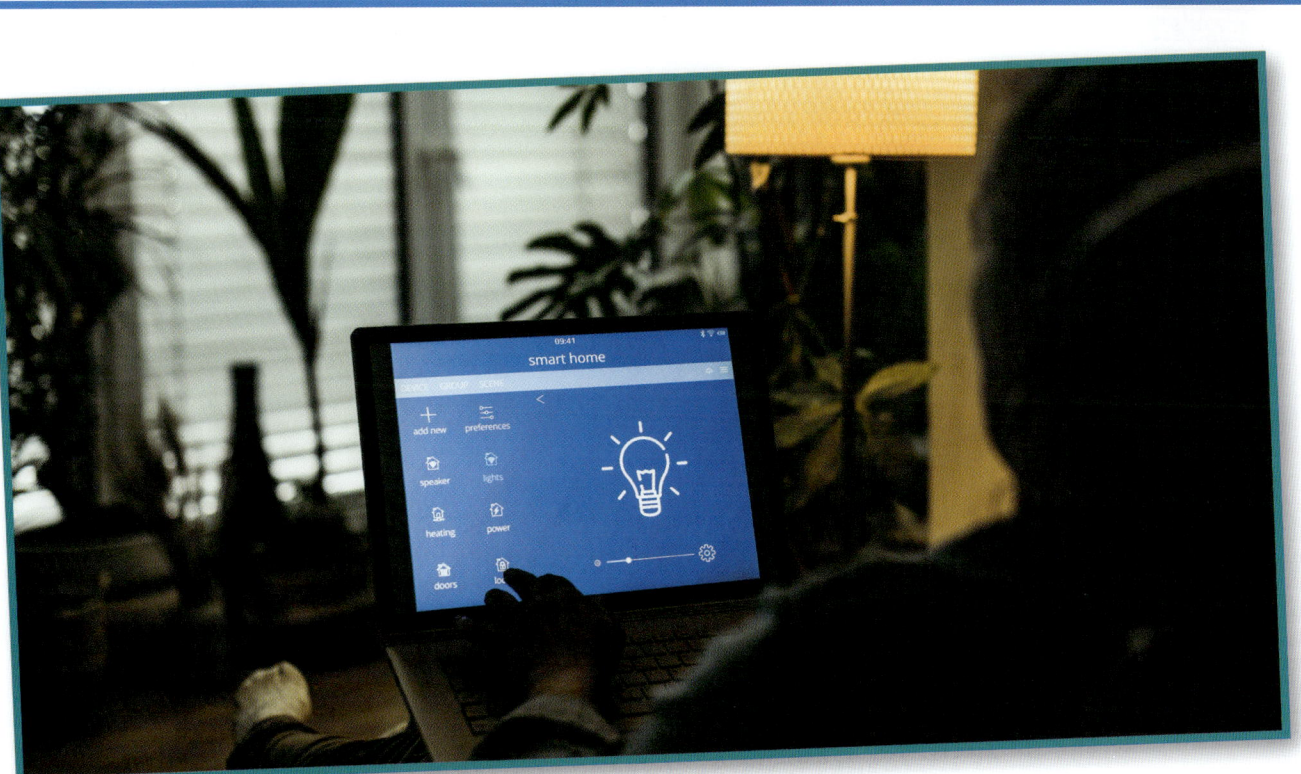

4 Computer systems

Stay safe!

When we use smart devices, data can be collected and stored on the internet about the things we use.

We need to be careful about who we share our data with and make sure we only share it with people and companies we trust.

Input devices send the computer information that it can understand.

What do you do with information to make it easy to understand?

Do you write it down in a certain way?

Do you have any special ways to help you understand and remember it?

Look what I can do!

- [ ] I can find input devices in computer systems.
- [ ] I know the difference between manual and automatic input devices.
- [ ] I can explain what the Internet of Things is and which everyday devices can connect to the internet.

4.3 Inputs and outputs around us

Project

Create your own smart bedroom

> You will need:
> a pencil and paper or a whiteboard pen and mini whiteboard, colouring pens or pencils

Work with a partner.

Design a smart bedroom of the future.

Think about the smart devices you would include in your bedroom.

What can they do when they are connected to the internet or other devices?

You can control all your lights using your phone.

Or you can have a wardrobe that uses the internet to check the weather and chooses your clothes every morning.

Draw a picture of your bedroom.

Label the smart devices that connect to the internet and other devices.

Add captions to explain how they work.

207

4 Computer systems

Check your progress

1. Software is the programs that computers use. True or false?

2. Which of these is a piece of hardware?

    A a drawing app

    B an email

    C a printer

3. Robots can only do what they have been programmed to do. True or false?

4. What are files used for in a computer system?

    A to stop the computer from getting a virus

    B to store information

    C to keep the computer up to date

5. Name three types of information that can be stored in computer files.

4.3 Inputs and outputs around us

Continued

6 Sofia has a motion sensor outside her back door that turns on a security light. What is a motion sensor?

7 Give an example of a digital device that is part of the Internet of Things.

8 Which of these contains an automatic input device?

A

B

C

209

Glossary

algorithm — a precise set of instructions — 11
Zara followed the algorithm to build a model.

antenna — a small pole that sends and receives information — 144
The wi-fi access device has an antenna on it to pick up signals from digital devices.

app — a computer program that does certain tasks — 173
The app on my brother's smartphone lets him play word games.

automatic input device — a device that is programmed once and can work by itself without people — 198
The light sensor in the streetlight is an automatic input device.

backdrop — the background in Scratch — 51
The backdrop of Sofia's program is a sports field.

bar chart — a chart with a solid coloured bar for each category; the longer the bar, the greater the value — 132
The bar chart shows that twice as many people voted for apples as for pears.

block palette — the place in Scratch where the command blocks are — 55
Zara clicked on the 'Control' menu in the block palette.

bug — an error in a program or algorithm — 52
The bug in the Scratch program made the sprite go the wrong way.

cell	box in a spreadsheet where data can be entered	119
	Marcus wrote a heading in the first cell in the spreadsheet.	
cipher	an algorithm that changes text into a secret code so that it is more difficult to read or understand	158
	We use a cipher to disguise the data.	
collect	to bring things together	106
	We collect data by asking questions.	
column	a group of cells in a spreadsheet that go downwards	119
	A spreadsheet has rows and columns.	
combine	to put two or more things together to make one thing	78
	Arun is going to combine two command blocks into one command block.	
command block	an instruction in Scratch that tells a computer what to do	48
	Sofia used the wait command block in her program.	
computer system	a computer and all the hardware connected to it	173
	There are lots of computer systems in my school.	
concise	giving clear instructions with as few words as possible	32
	A concise algorithm uses repeat instructions to reduce the number of instructions.	
costume	the way a sprite looks in Scratch	53
	The elephant sprite's costume shows it standing on three legs.	

data	a piece of data is a fact – it can be a word, number or picture	39
	Arun collected data about his classmates' favourite films.	
debug	to look for and correct errors in an algorithm or computer program	31
	We will debug our program because it isn't working properly.	
decode	understand the meaning of something	158
	Arun decodes the message from Sofia.	
download	to move information from one computer to another computer, usually using the internet	15
	Sofia downloads a file to her computer.	
editing	changing something	15
	Zara edits her algorithm to make it better.	
factory	a place where things are made	188
	The people in the factory work alongside machines to make cars.	
file	saved information that we can open on a computer	147
	Zara saves her file on the school server.	
format	the way information is shown	126
	Marcus asked Zara to format the numbers as dollars in the spreadsheet.	
hard drive	the part of a computer where data is stored	180
	The hard drive on the laptop was filled with photos.	
hardware	extra parts added to a computer that make a computer system	172
	A mouse is a piece of hardware.	
hat blocks	Scratch command blocks that tell the computer when to start a program	49
	A hat block has a round top to show that command blocks cannot be added above it.	

icon	a small picture	122
	The icon for choosing a sprite in Scratch is a cat's face.	
import	to copy or move something from one place to another	88
	Zara is going to import the file from the micro:bit to the computer.	
initialisation	a way to make sure things are changed so they are how they looked at the start	69
	Marcus used initialisation to make the cat in his program move back to where it started.	
input	information that is sent into something or information that tells us to do something	36
	Our teacher clapping his hands is an input which tells us it's time to start packing our things away.	
internet	a network of many computers connected together across the world	150
	All of the school computers are connected to the internet.	
Internet of Things	when everyday things such as fridges and televisions are connected to the internet	201
	The smart doorbell on my house is part of the Internet of Things.	
interpret	to try to understand what something means	107
	Sofia wants to interpret the graph the teacher gave her.	
LEDs	light-emitting diodes, which are lights that work well and last a long time	88
	Arun makes patterns by turning the LEDs on the micro:bit on and off.	

local area network	a computer network that connects digital devices in a building or group of buildings	147
	There is a local area network in the school that connects all the computers.	
logical thinking	a way of thinking or explaining something in a sensible way	18
	Sofia used logical thinking when she checked that she had everything she needed before she started the science experiment.	
machine	a device with some moving parts that uses power to do a job	188
	A robot vacuum cleaner is a type of machine.	
manual input device	a device where the inputs are controlled by a person using their hands	197
	A computer mouse is an example of a manual input device.	
micro:bit	a small computer	87
	You will learn to program a BBC micro:bit.	
motion sensor	a digital device that can tell when something moves in front of it	185
	The motion sensor sensed movement and sent a message to open the door.	
off-screen	not on a screen	87
	Some programs make things happen off-screen, like turning lights on or off.	
outputs	what happens when instructions are followed – the end result	41
	The output of Marcus's algorithm was that all his clothes were put away neatly.	
precise	clear and correct, with exact information	19
	Sophia's precise algorithm helped Arun to easily find her house.	

prediction	something you think will happen, based on what you already know	21
	I made a prediction that the sprite would jump up three times.	
present	to show something to someone	132
	Marcus used his computer to present his project.	
program	a list of instructions that makes a computer do a task	47
	You can use a program to make a drawing.	
repeat	to do something over and over again	31
	Arun made the sprite repeat moving from left to right.	
robot	a digital device that does a job without lots of help from humans	184
	The farm uses a robot to look for weeds.	
row	a group of cells in a spreadsheet that go across	120
	A spreadsheet is organised into rows and columns.	
'say' command	a command block in Scratch that adds a speech bubble to a sprite	61
	Sofia added a 'say' command to make her sprite say "Hello!".	
Scratch	a programming language	47
	Marcus made a program in Scratch.	
script area	the place in Scratch where command blocks can be joined together	50
	Arun made two programs in the script area.	
search engine	a program that lets you find things on the World Wide Web	151
	I use a search engine to find information about lions for my project.	
select	to choose something	112
	Zara selects her favourite film to write about in her school report.	

sensor	**a digital device that checks and records data**	**185**
	A light sensor tells the computer when to turn the lights on or off.	
server	**a computer that provides services such as programs and storage to other computers**	**147**
	I saved my work on the school server.	
services	**things like software and storage that a computer can access on another computer**	**146**
	The computer used the services on another computer to save files.	
simulator	**a version of a device or machine that lets people test something without using the real thing**	**96**
	Marcus used the micro:bit simulator to check his program before he downloaded it to the micro:bit.	
software	**the programs a computer uses**	**173**
	Sofia used messaging software to chat with Marcus one night.	
spreadsheet	**a type of program or document where data can be entered in rows and columns**	**119**
	Marcus used a spreadsheet to record data about his friends' favourite animals.	
sprite	**the object or character a program controls**	**52**
	Zara added a cat sprite to her program.	
stage area	**the place in Scratch where you can see a program running**	**48**
	Sofia ran her program in the stage area in Scratch.	
tasks	**pieces of work**	**24**
	Arun had to do five tasks to complete his program.	

toolbox	the place in MakeCode where all the commands blocks for writing a micro:bit program can be found	94
	Sofia found the command block she wanted in the toolbox.	
USB cable	a cable that joins a computer to another device	9 (Micro:bit document)
	Marcus used the USB cable to connect the micro:bit to the computer.	
'wait' command	a command block in Scratch which pauses the program that is running	55
	Arun used a wait command to pause his dinosaur sprite.	
web browser	software that allows us to view web pages on the internet	151
	Arun opened the web browser so that he could look at a website about music.	
wi-fi access point	a digital device that lets computers connect to a network without wires	144
	It is important that my laptop is near a wi-fi access point.	
World Wide Web	connected web pages and documents that can be viewed using a web browser	150
	I used the World Wide Web to find out how to look after hamsters.	

Acknowledgements

The authors and publishers acknowledge the following sources of copyright material and are grateful for the permissions granted. While every effort has been made, it has not always been possible to identify the sources of all the material used, or to trace all copyright holders. If any omissions are brought to our notice, we will be happy to include the appropriate acknowledgements on reprinting.

Thanks to the following for permission to reproduce images:

Unit 1 AndreaMPhoto/GI; Prostock-Studio/GI; Feifei Cui-Paoluzzo/GI; Blanchi Costela/GI; Spanteldotru/GI(x2); Peter Cade/GI; Emely/GI; Kali9/GI; Colin Hawkins/GI; Peter Dazeley/GI; Helen Camacaro/GI; AleksandarNakic/GI; Maca and Naca/GI; Sean Justice/GI; Jose Luis Pelaez Inc/GI; Martin Barraud/GI; Glow Images/GI; Dobrila Vignjevic/GI; Josephine Artois/GI; Image Source/GI; M-Production/GI; SolStock/GI; Marko Geber/GI; Praetorianphoto/GI; Klaus Vedfelt/GI; Jorg Greuel/GI; Fancy Yan/GI; PixelCatchers/GI; Marianna armata/GI; Mikroman6/GI; Stan Honda/GI; Alexis Rosenfeld/GI; Baona/GI; Jose Luis Pelaez Inc/GI; SDI Productions/GI; Krisanapong Detraphiphat/GI; Yoshiyoshi Hirokawa/GI; Filo/GI; Izusek/GI; Lisegagne/GI; Fstop123/GI; Thana Prasongsin/GI; Dilok Klaisataporn/GI; **Unit 2** Jayk7/GI; AndreyPopov/GI; Mokuden-photos/GI; Maria Fedotova/GI; Cavan Images/GI; Blend Images - Todd Wright/GI; DonNichols/GI; FatCamera/GI; Tomekbudujedomek/GI; momentimages/GI; Fat Camera/GI; Tetra Images/GI; Rudy Sulgan/GI; Tim Grist Photography/GI; Jonathan Kirn/GI; Monkey Business Images/GI; Martin Barraud/GI; Jose Luis Pelaez Inc/GI; Image Source/GI; Stefan Cristian Cioata/GI; Fuse/GI; **Unit 3** Ktsdesign/GI; popovaphoto/GI; Iain Lawrie/GI; Johner Images/GI; Juffin/GI; Setthaphat Dodchai/GI; Alexsl/GI; Sweetym/GI; MoMo Productions/GI; Busakorn Pongparnit/GI; Yuichiro Chino/GI; Tetra Images-Mike Kemp/GI; B.S.P.I./GI; Peter Dazeley/GI; ZenitX/GI; Johner Images/GI; Andersen Ross Photography Inc/GI; Blend Images - LWA/ Dann Tardif/GI; Klaus Vedfelt/GI; deepblue4you/GI; **Unit 4** Eugen Gheorghiu/GI; Thai Liang Lim/GI; Adha Ghazali/GI; Caia Image/GI; Photobuay/GI; Maskot/GI; Yuichiro Chino/GI; Humberto Ramirez/GI; Catherine McQueen/GI; Digital Art/GI; Katrina Wittkamp/GI; Ariel Skelley/GI; Vchal/GI; Hohl/GI; Stocktrek Images/GI; Monty Rakusen/GI; Ullstein bild/GI; Bogdanhoda/GI; Watchara Phomicinda/MediaNews Group/The Press-Enterprise via GI; Prasit photo/GI; Jean-Pierre Clatot/GI; wundervisuals/GI; Fine Art Images/Heritage Images via GI; Georgijevic/GI; Oscar Wong/GI; Roberto Jimenez Mejias/GI; Anthony Boulton/GI; Yevgen Romanenko/GI; Rouzes/GI; Yevgen Romanenko/GI; Joe daniel price/GI; Ryan McVay/GI; Koiguo/GI; Burwellphotography/GI; Bruev/GI; Tetra Images/GI; Ilbusca/GI; Wang Yukun/GI; D3sign/GI; Tara Moore/GI; Nastasic/GI; Janaka Dharmasena/GI; Alexander Spatari/GI; Westend61/GI; AzmanJaka/GI; Xia yuan/GI; Sean Gladwell/GI; Suparat Malipoom/GI; Rouzes/GI; **Using the Micro:bit** SDI Productions/GI

Key GI = Getty Images

Cover illustration by Pablo Gallego (Beehive Illustration)

Scratch is a project of the Scratch Foundation, in collaboration with the Lifelong Kindergarten Group at the MIT Media Lab. It is available for free at https://scratch.mit.edu

Illustrations and photos showing the BBC Micro:bit are created and used with permission from the Micro:bit Educational Foundation

Screenshots from Microsoft Excel are used with permission from Microsoft